Praise for
Plain Wisdom

"A treasure chest, for sure… The wisdom in these stories is time-tested and true—plain and simple."

—KAREN KINGSBURY, *New York Times* best-selling
author of *Unlocked* and *Shades of Blue*

"A fascinating comparison between two starkly different ways of life."

—DONALD B. KRAYBILL, author of *The Riddle
of Amish Culture*

"A beautiful weaving of the lives of two very different women drawn together through their bond of faith and love of family. Their intertwining stories offer both timeless wisdom and sincere encouragement to inspire all women to learn from one another's experiences. You will enjoy their honesty, their humor, and their life lessons as well as some of their delicious recipes! Cindy and Miriam bring us back to the place where our hearts long to go—a place of simplicity and truth."

—KAROL LADD, author of *The Power of a
Positive Woman*

"*Plain Wisdom* provides a beautiful glimpse into the lives of my longtime friend Cindy Woodsmall and her Amish friend Miriam Flaud. Though separated by the modern world and Old Order Amish customs, they have a living faith that bonds them and invites us to embrace our experiences with greater hope, delight, and laughter."

—DR. ALAN WEATHERLY, senior pastor of Asbury
United Methodist Church, Madison, Alabama

"Cindy Woodsmall and Miriam Flaud have the unique ability to marry two very different lifestyles in a masterful way by focusing on their similarities in faith and in daily life. Their chapters are easily digested in short pages designed for busy women—be they Amish or English. I loved savoring the wisdom in this book as well as the mouth-watering recipes. Written with the true insight of women who have been there, *Plain Wisdom* is a serious guide to life that doesn't take itself too seriously...and offers something for every woman."

—ELLIE KAY, author of *The 60-Minute Money Workout*

PLAIN
WISDOM

Other Books by Cindy Woodsmall

Ada's House series
The Hope of Refuge
The Bridge of Peace
(*The Harvest of Grace*, coming in fall 2011)

The Sound of Sleigh Bells

Sisters of the Quilt series
When the Heart Cries
When the Morning Comes
When the Soul Mends

CINDY WOODSMALL
& MIRIAM FLAUD

PLAIN WISDOM

AN INVITATION
into AN AMISH HOME
and the HEARTS *of* TWO WOMEN

WATERBROOK
PRESS

Plain Wisdom
Published by WaterBrook Press
12265 Oracle Boulevard, Suite 200
Colorado Springs, Colorado 80921

ISBN 978-0-307-45934-3
ISBN 978-0-307-45935-0 (electronic)

Copyright © 2011 by Cindy Woodsmall

Cover design by Mark D. Ford; cover photos: women on bench by Jim Celuch; background
by Dale Yoder

Published in the United States by WaterBrook Multnomah, an imprint of the Crown Publishing
Group, a division of Random House Inc., New York.

WATERBROOK and its deer colophon are registered trademarks of Random House Inc.

Library of Congress Cataloging-in-Publication Data
Woodsmall, Cindy.
  Plain wisdom : an invitation into an Amish home and the hearts of two women / Cindy
Woodsmall and Miriam Flaud. — 1st ed.
      p. cm.
  Includes bibliographical references (p.   ).
  ISBN 978-0-307-45934-3 — ISBN 978-0-307-45935-0 (electronic)
  1. Christian women—Religious life. 2. Amish women—Religious life. I. Flaud, Miriam.
II. Title.
  BV4527.W6235 2011
  277.3'083082—dc22

                         2010044303

Printed in the United States of America
2011—First Edition

10 9 8 7 6 5 4 3 2 1

Special Sales
Most WaterBrook Multnomah books are available at special quantity discounts when purchased
in bulk by corporations, organizations, and special-interest groups. Custom imprinting or
excerpting can also be done to fit special needs. For information, please e-mail SpecialMarkets@
WaterBrookMultnomah.com or call 1-800-603-7051.

From Miriam:

*To my awesome family: my husband, Daniel, and my children,
David, Jacob, Mervin, Michael, Amanda, and Mark.
To my wonderful daughters-in-law: Martha, Naomi, and Miriam.
To my precious grandchildren: Jolaine, Michael, Timothy,
Mervin, and J. R.
My love for all of you knows no bounds.*

*To my sisters, whom I love,
and to my friends—both Amish and English alike—
I cherish each of you.*

From Cindy:

*To Dad, Kathy, Leston, and Mark.
If we'd known then what we know now, we'd have
cherished each other more.
Our yesterdays are gone. Our tomorrows may never be.
But your indelible fingerprints are all over my heart,
at least until I reach eternity.
To my agent, Steve Laube.
I came to you with a heart's desire…and you heard me.
You counseled, cautioned, and encouraged—every word
wise and helpful.
You've poured years of support into helping Miriam and me
bring Plain Wisdom to fruition.*

*From the book's title, writing style, pacing, and voice
to the idea for the cover, your creative and technical guidance
is in every part of this work.*

CONTENTS

THE RHYTHM OF LIFE

TIMELESS BEGINNINGS

CHALLENGES GREAT AND SMALL

LAUGHTER IN ODD PLACES

BEAUTY, ASHES, AND THINGS BETWEEN

In His Hands

The Shape of Tomorrow

INTRODUCTION

In 2001 Miriam and I lived seven hundred miles apart geographically—but a century apart by customs. Miriam is an Old Order Amish woman trying to keep the Old Ways and avoid modernization. I am a typical American woman trying to keep up with the constant changes in technology while meeting the expectations of society, church, parents, and peers. We didn't know each other, but we had a mutual friend, and because of her, Miriam and I talked on the phone occasionally and shared letters regularly.

When Miriam invited me to visit her in 2002, I had no way of knowing how much we'd have in common. As our friendship grew, we began to realize that we've had many of the same life experiences, and we have approached them in faith and with some trepidation. Between us, we've given birth to nine babies—five we've ushered into adulthood; the others are now older teens or preteens. And both of us are still standing. Our cultural differences are vast; the more time I spend with Miriam, the more I realize just how different. Yet our methods for emotionally and spiritually dealing with life and work are remarkably similar.

In the visits since 2002, as we sat together, hedged in by her lilac bushes and sipping on coffee, a dream began to grow inside us. We wanted to share with other women our victories and defeats, what had and hadn't worked for us, and to encourage them by being real and vulnerable. Our friendship has shown us that whatever culture we live in, successes are possible…and failures are inevitable, but they're never final when placed in His hands.

As women we easily believe in the worth of a newborn, who can give nothing and takes much. We hold fast to hope for our children's future, even for those teens who fight us every step of the way. We can see our friends' lives through the eyes of faith. Yet when we think of ourselves, we often wallow in unforgiveness, self-loathing, and feelings of inadequacy.

Our desire is to help you embrace the beauty of the life God has given you. We wrote *Plain Wisdom* to encourage you to accept yourself, forgive yourself, challenge yourself, laugh at yourself, and, most important, see yourself through God's eyes of love. For when you do, you will find the freedom to truly enjoy your life.

Plain Wisdom is a collection of events in our lives—from early childhood to just a few months ago—and lessons we've learned, insights we've discovered, words of wisdom, Amish recipes, pictures of the Amish culture, and even a touch of Amish and "Englischer," or English (non-Amish), humor. In some cases we draw the lessons from our stories; at other times we'll let the events speak for themselves, allowing the Holy Spirit to whisper to readers' hearts through the details.

Our hope and prayer are that these memories will encourage and strengthen you as you create memories within your friend and family circles.

Meet Miriam and Cindy

> Then Peter opened his mouth, and said, Of
> a truth I perceive that God is no respecter of
> persons: but in every nation he that feareth
> him, and worketh righteousness, is accepted
> with him.
>
> —Acts 10:34–35

From Miriam

In the early eighteenth century, my ancestors crossed the Atlantic Ocean, traveling from Switzerland to America to escape persecution for their religious beliefs. As an Old Order Amish woman, I call myself the "Plain" part of *Plain Wisdom*. (Perhaps that makes Cindy the "Wisdom" part.)

I was born in St. Mary's County in southern Maryland, the third of seven children. When I was a year old, we moved to Adams County, Pennsylvania. My home was always filled with family from both my mom's and my dad's sides. Then, when I was eleven, my parents bought a farm in the neighboring Franklin County. Today my husband and I live on the farm where he grew up, which is within walking distance of my parents' place.

When one is born into an Amish household, he or she is expected to remain Amish and eventually join the church. The youth are encouraged to join the faith in their teen years. For me, like for most Amish youth, the question wasn't, would I join? but rather, when would I take that step?

So when the desire and the appropriate age came together, I, along with six other young women and six young men, took the first steps by attending instruction classes. A church leader teaches instruction classes, and, similar to courses held by other faiths, the purpose of instruction is to clarify the founding principles and scriptures of our faith. The lessons begin in late spring and continue throughout the summer. Meanwhile, I was courted by a handsome young man named Daniel Flaud, who was from the same youth group and church. The following year we were married. Eighteen months later we were blessed with our first son. As the years went by, we had four more sons and a daughter. Now, nearly thirty years later, our family has welcomed three daughters-in-law and five grandchildren.

I've enjoyed my life inside one of the most structured societies in the United States. I haven't always known what to do, agreed with the rules, or handled situations with wisdom. But I've experienced the abundant joys as well as the occasional frustration our lifestyle brings.

Often when we meet people, we see our own lives differently—perhaps better in some ways and worse in others. Sometimes we choose to stay inside our familiar circles so we can avoid the discomforts that are a part of building new friendships. Cindy's world was so very different than mine. Sophisticated. Filled with technology. And by my Plain standards, it was worldly. I invite you to come along as I prepared to welcome her into my home.

From Cindy

Some of you know me as the author of fiction books with Amish settings and characters. But, like Miriam, my family roots trace back to Europe (specifically to Scotland), and my ancestors landed in America in the mid–seventeen hundreds. I was born in Washington DC, the youngest child in a family of four. When my parents were growing up, their family lives were tough, and they had almost no support. But when they married in their teenage years, they were determined to beat the odds and make a success out of their lives.

My family moved frequently when I was growing up. My dad would buy an old home in need of repair, and he and Mom would fix it up while living in it. Then they would sell it, and the process would start all over again. No matter where we lived, my vivid imagination constantly wove fictional stories of family life, romance, and conflict.

The summer between my eighth- and ninth-grade years in school, my family moved from Maryland to Alabama. Because of that move, I eventually met and married Tommy. A few years after that, we had our first son, and I became a full-time homemaker. Two years later I gave birth to our second son. I homeschooled our two boys through middle school, and we welcomed a third son into our home in 1994.

Throughout the years my mind had continued to devise fictional stories, but I was never willing to invest time in writing them. The story ideas were ceaseless, and, in hopes of quieting them, I began writing as a hobby in 1999. In 2002 I attended my first writers' conference[1] and then fell in love with the whole writing process.

I've enjoyed the freedom and opportunity granted to American women—whether it was choosing what church to attend, how to school our children, or what career path to take. But like Miriam, I haven't always known what to do, agreed with all the rules that bound me, or handled every situation with wisdom. I, too, have experienced the abundant joys of my lifestyle as well as the frustrations.

One of the great blessings in my life is having been invited into Miriam's home and into her life. Neither of us could have imagined what that initial visit would lead to as I anxiously went from my world into hers.

Come, travel with me as I entered her world for the first time.

WHEN PLAIN MEETS FANCY

Two are better than one, because they have a
good return for their work: If one falls down,
his friend can help him…But pity the man
who falls and has no one to help him up!

—ECCLESIASTES 4:9–10, NIV

From Miriam
2002

The sound of a push reel mower could be heard from my kitchen window
as my son Mark made the last few rounds in the front yard. We had been
looking forward to this day for months. Cindy Woodsmall and her son
Tyler were expected to arrive at any minute. While I chopped veggies for
the salad for that night's supper, my daughter, Amanda, hurriedly swept
the kitchen one more time as we anxiously watched the road for our
company.

Cindy and I had chosen the second week in June because my husband,
Daniel, was planning to be in Maine that week on a timber-framing job.
We thought this would give us lots of chat time—just the moms and our
six children, three of which had full-time summer jobs. Daniel would be
here when she arrived, but I knew he'd have to leave soon afterward. As
the time of her arrival drew near, I found myself wishing my husband
could stay. He's the social one, able to maintain interesting conversations
with anyone. Suddenly I went from being a little nervous to a lot nervous.

What if she came all this way and was disappointed not only in my ability to hold a reasonable conversation but also in me as a person? We'd shared letters and long phone conversations, but what if I fell way short of her expectations once we were together?

After their arrival Daniel kept the conversation lively for about an hour, but then he had to leave. The house grew silent and the conversation became stilted the moment he left. Cindy and I spent the afternoon trying to break the ice, and then that evening we gathered around the dining room table to share a meal. My still-in-the-nest children—three in their teens and two elementary-school age—are usually quite talkative at dinnertime, but they were awfully quiet that evening. With my husband gone, I took my place in his chair at the head of the table, and I felt very uncomfortable doing so. I tried to think of things to say but found myself lost in a sea of wishing that Daniel were home.

Cindy and Tyler were very quiet also as everyone passed the food around the table and filled their plates. Cindy put some salad on her plate, so I handed her the salad dressing. A moment later I heard her gasp in dismay. A quick glance told me she'd mistaken our regular salad dressing bottle for a squeeze type, resulting in a plate full of food covered in salad dressing. Poor girl, I felt so bad for her. Before me stood the opportunity to continue being extremely polite or just to be me. I chose to be me. Leaning in, I quietly said, "I'm sorry, Cindy, but the Amish are forbidden to have the handy squeeze bottles."

Her eyes grew as big as saucers, her mouth formed a perfect little O. For a few seconds she actually thought I was serious. Then we burst into laughter, and the ice broke. Completely. From that moment on, our days flew by. We talked freely over coffee as the sun rose the next morning; we laughed together as she tried to do chores the Amish way; we cried together while sharing our heartaches; we watched our boys ride horses and foot scooters while they chatted ceaselessly; and we gave them freedom to fish from a nearby dock without our hovering (but we watched from inside the house). And when they didn't catch enough for supper, we quietly baked frozen fish sticks without their ever realizing what we'd done. After the sun went down, we made s'mores over a fire in the backyard.

All too soon the week came to an end, and it was time for Cindy and Tyler to go back home to their world. It had been a great week, and I feasted on the memories until it was time for her to visit again.

From Cindy

Miriam's garden still needed more weeding as the sun slid below the horizon, taxing my ability to distinguish between weeds and produce. Laundry on the clothesline flapped in the evening breeze, and supper dishes sat in the sink, reminding Miriam and me that we'd moved too slowly through the chores as I'd spent the day learning to handle the summertime responsibilities of an Amish woman.

Tomorrow Miriam's morning would begin before daylight as she prepared breakfasts, packed lunches, and passed around clean clothes for her three oldest sons. The boys had already graduated from the eighth grade in their one-room schoolhouse and now apprenticed full-time within the Amish community.

After crossing the lawn without the assistance of floodlights or lampposts, we checked on our youngest children. They sat around a campfire with one of Miriam's teen sons, roasting marshmallows and making s'mores. The fireflies they'd caught earlier glowed in a jar beside them, waiting to be released.

Miriam and I went separate ways to finish the day's work, she to the clothesline and I to the kitchen. As I washed dishes by a kerosene lamp, I could see her silhouette bathed in moonlight as she collected the last of the laundry. Wiping sweat from my face, I heard her call to the children, telling them it was almost bedtime.

While Miriam's children doused the campfire, my son made his way inside, washed up at the mud sink, and waited for me to escort him through the dark home. I took the kerosene lamp, and we climbed the wooden, spiral stairway. A mule brayed, cows mooed, and bullfrogs from a nearby pond croaked—all quite loudly. I smiled, but I knew that before sleep came, I'd long for some electrical device to block out the sounds of the farm and stir the summer's humid air.

Today I look back to that first visit eight years ago. As a resident of Georgia, I had doubted I could find a way to talk to someone who was part of the Old Order Amish life, but I had a story in my heart, and I needed an inside view of Plain living to be able to write it.

Growing up in Maryland, I'd had an Amish Mennonite best friend, and our adventures—along with the reservations our parents had concerning our friendship—had sparked my desire to write about the joys and difficulties of relationships, both within the Amish community and with outsiders. But as with many writers, I didn't actually begin to put those stories on paper until decades later. Long before I sat down to write, my family had moved away, and my Amish Mennonite friend and I had lost all contact.

But in 2001, Linda, a friend who had worked at an Amish birthing center and as an EMT among the Amish, knew of Miriam and had connected the two of us. This connection began the long-distance relationship. More than a year into this relationship, Miriam invited me to visit her place.

This was the first of what has become at least a yearly visit. I've been greatly blessed by the friendship with Miriam and her family. She and I marvel that forging a friendship was easier than either of us expected. It took us one evening, really, and a plate full of salad dressing.

THE RHYTHM
OF LIFE

A Sense of
Community

On my first visit to Miriam's, our mutual friend, Linda, picked Tyler and me up in Harrisburg, Pennsylvania, near the train station. We headed west, out of the busyness of the city, and before long we were traveling down winding roads that carried us to more sparsely populated areas.

Sunlight splashed across the mountains and valleys like a spotlight revealing props on a stage. The fields were lush with half-grown hay that swayed in the breeze. As we drew closer to Miriam's home, Linda pointed out the fenced areas that belonged to the Flaud family. Cows stood in wide pastures, horses grazed in a small field near the barn, and rows of clothing hung on lines, snapping in the wind as they soaked up the fresh scent of spring air.

Linda pulled onto the dirt-and-gravel driveway and parked. When we got out of the car, the heat smacked us with mid-June temperatures in the nineties. The double-wide wooden doors to the red and white barn stood open, and a quick glance revealed empty milking stalls. A silo attached to the barn towered higher than the trees surrounding the two-century-old brick farmhouse. A large garden in her backyard was lined with rows of vegetables.

Linda, Tyler, and I walked up a concrete sidewalk. Miriam and her husband, Daniel, greeted us at the door before we had a chance to knock.

Their friendly smiles were more beautiful in person than I'd imagined during the months of speaking to them on the phone.

I stepped into their Old Order Amish home, noticing half a dozen things all at once. The mud sink that sat mere feet from the front door. Straw hats hanging on a hatrack. Boots and waders, obviously used for milking cows, lined up neatly along the wall. A family-sized thermos on the kitchen counter with rows of glasses nearby. (I later learned this is Miriam's way of providing her children with plenty of cold water on hot days without their needing to constantly open her gas-powered refrigerator.)

Without electricity the rich beauty of sunlight filtering through the canopy of trees brought a soft green glow to the rooms, and a breeze cooled the house in spite of the sweltering temperature outside. The mouth-watering aroma of freshly made desserts and percolated coffee filled the air.

While growing up in Maryland, I'd been in Plain homes but never in an Old Order Amish home. I'd like to share with you some of what I've learned, but at times you may wonder why I'm not going into more detail. The Old Order Amish are very private people, and true friends would never share anything publicly that would make each other uncomfortable. This book offers an invitation into an Amish home. That's a cherished invite, and as a guest we'll enjoy the warmth, honesty, good food, and insights while minding our manners by not asking for more. I hope that's where our heart is whenever we enter anyone's home. Come. Let's enjoy our visit.

❧❀❧

An Old Order Amish community is usually made up of homes scattered throughout the hillsides of a farming country. Ohio, Pennsylvania, and Indiana have the highest population of Old Order Amish, but they live in other states too, including Maine, Missouri, Kentucky, Minnesota, and Colorado.

An Amish district has approximately twenty-five families, and each district has three preachers and a deacon. When a district has more than thirty to thirty-five families—most often due to children becoming adults, getting married, and forming their own homes—the church leaders will begin a new district. Keeping the number of households limited in each district is necessary when you consider that church is held in someone's home every other Sunday, a family-style meal is served afterward, and during the school year, one teacher works with students in all eight grades.

Today most Amish children attend classes in a one- or two-room schoolhouse. Generally they are taught by a young Amish woman; although men can teach, few choose to do so. Just as I cannot opt for my children to attend school outside of our district, the Amish cannot opt to attend a church or school outside the district in which they live. However, if a new district has not yet established an Amish school, the children may attend the closest Amish or Mennonite school. In some areas Amish children attend public school because their community is unable to build their own school. The Amish receive no government support for their schools, so the costs of constructing a building, supplying it with desks, books, and equipment, and paying a teacher's salary can be too much.

Although the Old Order Amish may take advantage of some modern conveniences, like hiring a driver to take them to a job site or a doctor's appointment or a local Wal-Mart, those things are done sparingly, and they are not necessary to sustaining their way of life. Because the Amish community has farmers, builders, craftsmen, blacksmiths, church leaders, midwives, and teachers, they are fairly self-sufficient. Most Amish people are either self-employed or work for Amish relatives, with many young men carrying on the work of their forefathers.

When a young man turns fifteen, he begins an apprenticeship as a craftsman or farmer, often under his father or an uncle. The girls apprentice under their mothers, learning about sewing, gardening, canning, and tending to little ones. The girls also work at local grocery stores, markets, restaurants, and bakeries.

When an Amish man owns a business, it's his responsibility to hire as many Amish men as he can; this tradition keeps the Amish from losing its young people to the outside world and helps promote unity and a sense of community. It also helps sustain the independence of the community. If a man's business is successful enough, he may find a facet of that trade that can be turned into a separate business for another family to start.

In addition to similar interests, skills, locality, culture, and heritage, the Amish have also preserved their sense of community by having their own language. They speak what is commonly referred to as Pennsylvania Dutch, although the word *Dutch* in this phrase has nothing to do with the Netherlands. The original word was *Deutsch,* which means "German." The Amish speak some High German (in church services) and Pennsylvania German (Pennsylvania Dutch), and after a certain age the children are taught English. This causes the children to feel closely connected to their community. When a non-Amish person speaks to young Amish children in English, the language may not make sense to them.

I enjoy spending time with Miriam's grandchildren. Since I don't have any of my own, I soak in their cuteness like a dry sponge in a bucket of water. But sometimes they look at me funny when I talk to them because they don't understand what I'm saying, and when I try to speak in Pennsylvania Dutch, I fail miserably. But one of Miriam's sons has become adept at listening to how I mispronounce their words, and he can usually help me. He always relates the correct pronunciation to a familiar English word so I know how the word should sound. Even my Southern accent doesn't thwart him, although it does make him laugh.

The Old Order Amish lifestyle is much more than what's easily seen—how they dress, travel by horse and buggy, and live without electricity. The true sense of living Old Order Amish is found in the close-knit lives of those who make up the Amish community.

From Miriam

This recipe is often brought to our many large gatherings. I don't know anyone who doesn't love it.

CHICKEN SPAGHETTI

1 chicken, cooked and chopped (about 2–3 cups)
1 pound spaghetti, cooked
1/2 cup chopped onion
1/2 cup chopped celery
pat of butter
1 cup chicken broth
1 cup milk
1 can condensed cream of mushroom soup
1 can condensed tomato soup
salt and pepper to taste
1/2 pound Velveeta cheese

Place cooked chicken and spaghetti in a container, and set aside. In a large pot sauté onions and celery in a pat of butter. Add broth, milk, and soups. Bring to a boil. Remove from the heat, and add chicken and spaghetti. Add salt and pepper as needed. Pour the mixture into a 9" x 13" greased or sprayed casserole dish. Cover with cheese. Bake at 350 degrees until it's heated thoroughly and the cheese has browned.

FINDING RHYTHM

> And God called the light day, and the
> darkness He called night. And there was
> evening and there was morning, one day.
>
> —GENESIS 1:5, NASB

From Miriam

Nature gives us the unexpected, but it also gives us rhythm. When God created the world, He designed the sun to rise in the east and set in the west at basically the same times each day, allowing for the seasonal changes. We can depend on our Creator for this rhythm day after day, week after week, year after year, as it has been since the beginning of time.

I look forward to each new season. When I grow weary of snow and cold, I am encouraged by knowing an end is in sight. Winter fades and spring begins. During those first few weeks of spring, I love the feel of the sun on my back and the warmth of garden dirt under my feet as I plant fresh seeds in the ground. In summer I enjoy having my children around more, even as the temperatures rise to scorching and the hot sun dries up the ground. By the time fall rolls around, my desire for warm weather and gardening has been fulfilled. Having plowed, planted, weeded, and harvested through spring, summer, and into late fall, I look forward again to the quieter indoor season of winter.

Knowing and trusting in God's rhythm helps me in many ways, and I use His rhythm to create my own. The rhythm of the day. The rhythm of the season. The rhythm of life.

From Cindy

The first time I entered the Amish world as an adult, I had traveled for eighteen hours by train, my son and I spending the night in a sleeper car. I couldn't sleep, so I pulled out my laptop and worked, glancing up every so often to take in the beauty of distant lights shining amid the dark towns.

I'd spent years honing the skill of multitasking, so working when I couldn't sleep made perfect sense. My life's goal seemed to be sharpening my ability to juggle more tasks using less time.

But when I stepped into my friend's Old Order Amish world, I found something I hadn't known I was missing: a sense of morning, noon, and night.

At home my mornings consisted of the same things as my middays, late afternoons, and evenings: the computer, e-mails, phone calls, writing, editing. The family chores had no boundary between morning and evening. I could move a load of clothes into the dryer just as easily at ten o'clock at night as I could at ten in the morning. E-mails were sent just as naturally before daylight as before bedtime. I woke each morning to the call of busyness, but I had lost the rhythm of the day—the tempo of sunshine filtering into my soul, listening to the birds wake, and breathing in the aroma of a day's fresh start.

In Miriam's world the uniqueness of morning, noon, and evening is too strong to miss. Laundry has to be washed and hung out early. Cows and horses need to be tended to before breakfast. Without electricity, navigating the home after the sun goes down brings a sense of closure to the day.

During my visit that week, I felt the rhythm and nuances of a day as the sun moved across the sky from east to west, and I began to mourn the years I'd been too busy to truly notice. I certainly knew when morning arrived each day, and I had a long list of morning things to accomplish, but electricity and natural gas provided me with an unnoticed shield.

Beyond the protection it had given me against the harshness of winter and summer, that shield had also blocked my senses and my soul from the beauty of feeling a day slide across the sky. Sipping a cup of coffee on the front porch each day couldn't solve the problem because it went deeper than how I spent a few minutes here and there. I've become so involved in *doing* life that I've acquired a type of tunnel vision in experiencing the days, months, and seasons.

As the Amish need to step inside our world from time to time to meet their needs—using a Realtor, seeing a specialist, or borrowing money from a bank—I want to find a way to step into theirs, to feel the pulse of each day even while living in my world.

Maybe We All Need a Green Thumb

But other [seed] fell into good ground, and
brought forth fruit, some an hundredfold,
some sixtyfold, some thirtyfold.

—Matthew 13:8

From Miriam

Early in 2009 my craft orders were piling up, and I was behind in my writing for *Plain Wisdom*. Although I'd set aside working on my crafts in order to write, I still had the items around me. The room was filled with baskets that I had lined with fabric and lids on which I had painted scenery. I make birdhouses from old boots, and after bending a discarded license plate in half, I use that as the roof. I have stacks of prints from scenery I've painted and the frames I put them in. And I hand piece and quilt wall hangings, often framing them in a set of wooden hames (curved pieces in a horse's collar). With all those supplies and *Plain Wisdom* calling to me, I still could not block out my other responsibilities and obligations by closing myself in that one room. With every telephone call or knock on my door, I'd lose my train of thought. Getting ahead with my crafting put me more behind in my writing, and vice versa.

One morning a friend stopped in, wanting my help with some serious issues. On the verge of frustration and feeling guilty for being so selfish with my time, I tried to reassure myself that I was doing the right thing by walking away from my work. This thought came to mind: in the garden of life, being successful isn't just about hoeing your own row but also about slowing down enough to help your brother hoe his row until he is caught up, then hoeing the rest of the field together.

From Cindy

My mother once told me that she always had flower beds while I was growing up and that she worked in them regularly. I believed her, but I didn't remember seeing any flowers or watching her plant them.

I do remember her working a vegetable garden. That was food, and I liked food. I remember her canning and freezing all sorts of fruits and vegetables. That impressed me too.

But flowers? They didn't do anything. Why work hard planting seeds to grow something you can only look at?

My lack of respect for her love of flowers included houseplants. Except for the aloe plant that I'd cut and apply to burns on occasion, I never understood the purpose of houseplants. So when she brought me several after I had my own home, I didn't honor her gift. I was nice when she gave them to me, but before long they were dying. It seemed wrong to let them die when she'd spent money on them, so I tried to keep them alive—gave them plenty of sun, water, fresh soil. But my efforts came too late. I'd already either baked them in the sun or drowned them in water. Or both.

When I confessed my failure to Mom, she laughed and said it was a fault she'd overlook. She assured me that one day I'd appreciate flowers and houseplants. I told her not to hold her breath. It became a running joke between us. Whenever a sibling asked her what gift I might like for Christmas or a birthday, she'd wink at me and say plants would be perfect! When we walked through the garden section of any store, she'd lovingly touch the plants and say they were calling my name.

One afternoon in May of 1998, I received a phone call saying that my healthy, sixty-eight-year-old mom had been outside planting flowers when she started feeling odd. Forty minutes later she died. I was in shock.

After the funeral, as my husband was backing out of the driveway to head for home, my sister hurried out to our car, toting a flat of three-inch seedlings with six different types of plants. "Someone gave these houseplants in lieu of flowers. Please take them with you. You know Mom would want you to have them."

Wondering if they'd survive the seven-hundred-mile trip home in a tightly packed vehicle with antsy children, I took them. Out of respect for my mom, I determined to do whatever it took to make sure these plants survived as long as possible.

The grieving process was long and hard, but keeping those plants alive and thriving brought healing. I've replanted them into larger containers four times so far. Now, twelve years later, each of those plants has its own large, ornate pot. Except in the wintertime, they sit on my back porch. How did I not see the beauty of plants before?

When my oldest son bought a home of his own a couple of years ago, I gave him shoots from the once-seedlings I'd received at his grandmother's funeral. He looked at me with a funny expression and said, "What do I want with houseplants? They aren't good for anything but sitting around and collecting dust...until they die."

At that moment I realized that the circle of my mom's passing on her love of plants to her family was not yet complete—and might not ever be.

THE UNEXPECTED

Be kindly affectioned one to another with
brotherly love; in honour preferring one another.

—ROMANS 12:10

From Cindy

The saying "Stop and smell the roses" has lost its impact through years of use, but its message is still true.

On one occasion, when my husband and I had two preschoolers, we took a three-hour road trip to visit my parents. Our budget was tight, and we didn't usually eat out, but we'd saved a little money so we could stop at a Cracker Barrel and have a nice breakfast.

After ordering we played checkers with our children and drew pictures on scrap paper—the typical things parents do to keep their balls of energy in check and content. I noticed a woman about ten years older than we were who was watching our every move, but I didn't think much about it. When it was time to pay the bill, the server said it had already been paid, including the tip. The server pointed to the table where that woman had been sitting just a few minutes earlier. She had told the server, "I used to have a family like that. Tell the parents to enjoy what they have while they can."

My heart wrenched when the server told us that. Perhaps she wasn't as young as she looked and her children were grown, leaving her alone and regretting that she hadn't used her time with them more wisely. Could she have lost her children in a divorce or to death? It became very clear that I might have only that day and that moment with my children.

But had I taken time to breathe in their joy and laughter, or was I rushing through the seasons life was giving me? Even now, more than twenty years later, my heart aches at the memory of her pain.

That incident has had a profound effect on my relationship with my husband and children. Since that day I have been more aware that any conversation with one of them could be my last one. Because of that, my anger is tempered, my disappointment is quenched, and my hope for tomorrow becomes a prayer.

From Miriam

Sometime ago Flaud Builders, our family business, built a boat shop in Maine for Bob and Ruth Ives. After spending a week with them constructing the timber frame, we grew quite fond of the admirable couple. Sadly, shortly after we finished the job, Ruth died of a brain tumor following a long, brave battle.

Later my husband and I, along with three other workers and their wives, decided to return to Maine to visit Bob. We pulled out our handwritten list of people who are willing to be hired drivers for the Amish. We know most of them well, so we knew who had a van that would seat all of us. Then we called to see who had the time and would be willing to make the twelve-hour trip, stay in the area until we were ready to leave, and drive us home again.

Once everything was arranged, we headed for Maine. When we had almost reached our destination, we decided to stop for a bite to eat so we wouldn't arrive just before mealtime. We had already left the main roads, so finding a restaurant wasn't going to be easy.

Hungry and weary of traveling, I didn't think I'd be too choosy, but when we drove up to a little diner, my heart sank. At first glance it appeared to be no more than an enclosed front porch, but they were open for business, so we went inside.

The place was small, but it was warm and clean, and the coffee smelled good. Our group split up and sat at several tables.

After I placed my order, I noticed the rest of the group chatting with a gentleman who had just come in. It's not unusual for strangers to approach us and ask where we're from—after all, we do look like we recently stepped off the *Mayflower*.

A few bites of my eggs Benedict, and I felt ashamed that I had doubted the place. My breakfast was delicious. My sister raved about hers as well, calling it outstanding.

When the waitress returned to refill our coffee, she told us the tall gentleman at the counter had picked up all our tabs! As we expressed our appreciation, he said he was familiar with the boat shop, was a friend of Bob Ives, and had known Ruth well. Then in a low voice he said, "This breakfast was from Ruth. If she were still alive, she would have insisted on making her guests breakfast."

My eyes welled with tears. I looked at my sister and said, "No wonder this meal tasted so good; it was made in heaven."

We all left there filled in more ways than one.

We received love from a stranger that day because Ruth would have given it to us if she had been here on earth. I felt as if Ruth had reached out to us, as if I'd received a hug from heaven. And the fresh insight of how God's love comes from heaven and fills us so that we can reach out and love others for Him became even clearer.

Since God's own Son was born in a barn, surely His angels can work in a humble little diner through a tall gentleman with an open heart.

ACROSS-THE-FIELD NOTES

Now the God of peace, that brought again
from the dead our Lord Jesus, that great
shepherd of the sheep, through the blood
of the everlasting covenant, make you perfect
in every good work to do his will, working
in you that which is wellpleasing in his sight,
through Jesus Christ; to whom be glory for
ever and ever. Amen.

—HEBREWS 13:20–21

From Miriam

The sunshine felt warm on my back as I bent to pick fresh green beans from my garden. In the distance I heard the rumble of an approaching team of horses. Looking up, I saw my husband's twin brother driving down the dusty field lane, most likely coming to help with the hay making.

When his two workhorses and cart reached the end of my garden, he stopped the rig and pulled a slip of white paper from his pocket. Probably a note from my sister Sarah, what we call an across-the-field note. As our husbands help each other with their crops, we pass notes back and forth through them, sharing recipes and generally staying in touch between visits.

Sarah recycles everything possible, so her notes are usually written on the back of discarded desk-calendar sheets, the kind with a scripture for each day. I always look forward to those little notes as well as the Bible verses. Many times that one little passage is just the right encouragement, inspiration, or discipline I need for the day.

I don't think this is a coincidence. God knows exactly what our needs will be long before we even realize we have them.

From Cindy

Whether learning at home or at public school, Tyler never enjoyed class time. He experienced a number of difficulties in his first two years of middle school. Soon after starting his third year of middle school, he began pushing me to homeschool him again.

I'd had sixteen years of experience in homeschooling, but at that juncture of life, I was in the middle of fulfilling publishing contracts for two novels. I couldn't juggle teaching Tyler while keeping up with my writing obligations. It would have been impossible even if he had been an independent learner, which at that time he wasn't.

I met with his teachers, and they expressed a number of concerns. His new friends at school were rough—some under house arrest, others not far behind. A rebellious attitude had begun to develop in Tyler. Self-destructive behavior was trying to creep into his heart as well.

I talked to my son about this, covered him in prayer, and sent him back to school.

What else could I do?

A few weeks later I was walking into church one Sunday morning, my mind on the next week's schedule and how I'd get everything done. Suddenly, from out of nowhere, I heard, *Get him out. Now.*

I couldn't imagine how I'd manage to homeschool Tyler and still meet my writing obligations. But I'd ignored God's direction on different issues in the past, and disobedience had come with a price, so I knew I had to heed His warning in order to steer clear of whatever danger was ahead.

With great trepidation I withdrew Tyler from school, ordered curriculum, and tried to hire a tutor. Not one applicant qualified.

For three weeks I woke at four every morning, wrote until nine, then started the school day. Tyler's attitude showed significant improvement. I, on the other hand, was more exhausted and stressed than I'd ever been. I had no clue how I was going to make my book deadlines. Something had to give. Since I was committed to homeschooling Tyler, the only option I could see was to back out of my publishing contracts.

Before telling my agent my decision, I talked to my pastor about our need for a tutor. He said he knew a man who might be willing to help. Later that week Dr. Lee came for an interview. He had several degrees, one in math. While waiting for God to open a door for him to become a pastor, he agreed to come to my home two days a week and work with Tyler on math. I found another qualified tutor who could come a few hours each week to teach history and science.

Dr. Lee was a soft-spoken man, and he saw Tyler's heart. He identified what was tripping him up, both in academics and in issues that had nothing to do with school.

Tyler finished the year with outstanding grades, and I managed to meet my two book deadlines. Just as we completed our school year, Dr. Lee's door of opportunity opened in another part of the country.

When the new school year approached, I gave Tyler the choice to stay home or return to school. He chose to return. He needed to be homeschooled for eighth grade, and he needed to return to public school the following year.

Tyler has become a better student and a better young man every year. Math clicks for him now. He gets good grades in his honors classes. He enjoys good friends and avoids bad ones. And he appreciates that God spoke up for him and that his parents did what it took to get him on track.

Before we even withdrew Tyler from school, God had a plan of success for both of us. But I wouldn't have discovered that if I hadn't dared to obey.

R-E-S-P-E-C-T

Being justified by his grace, we should be
made heirs according to the hope of eternal
life.

—TITUS 3:7

From Miriam

While my husband lined up our four little boys at the picnic table, I
handed out paper plates full of goodies. The local milk company was
sponsoring its annual picnic for milk producers and their families. Being
dairy farmers, with cows to milk twice a day, we don't get away very
often. So this event is always a treat for us.

A huge crowd had gathered, including the milk inspector. The sight
of him made me anxious. Two weeks prior to the picnic, our farm had
undergone its routine inspection. Similar to a restaurant inspector, a dairy
inspector comes with a long list of items to check and standards that must
be met. Failing to pass one of these inspections means the inspector may
refuse to accept a few days' worth of milk as a penalty…and all the milk
will be dumped down the drain. The inspector would have to return and
do another inspection before we could begin selling milk again.

While my husband had cut hay, I'd worked hard scrubbing the milk-
ers, the bulk tank, and the milk-house walls and windows. I'd scraped the
cow stalls and spread barn snow, a white lime sand used to freshen the
concrete floor. As far as I knew, everything should have passed the rigid
inspection.

But there we were at the picnic, and we hadn't received the results yet. Usually no news is good news, but the suspense still affected me. We'd probably passed, but by how much? And what else would we need to do for the next inspection? The thought of all my hard work kept running through my mind, and I began to feel as if I just couldn't take on that task again.

As I sat down to join my husband and sons, the inspector walked up to our table. He greeted my father-in-law, who is in partnership with us. When the man mentioned something about inspection results, I froze. But before he could finish his comment, my father-in-law interrupted. "Actually," he said, "I handed that job over to my son."

The inspector took a few steps down the table and greeted my husband. When he resumed his conversation about the inspection, Daniel seemed relieved to hand the possible wrath down to the next person. He said, "Well, that would be my wife's department."

The inspector looked at me. I held my breath, glad I was sitting down.

He extended his arm to shake hands with me, and then he said, "Congratulations, Mrs. Flaud. Not only did you pass inspection, but you got an outstanding score of 99 percent!"

I didn't want to gloat. I prayed not to, and yet...I'm human.

From Cindy

The journey from stay-at-home mom to author was a quiet one. While writing my first novel, I worked long hours at the same place where I'd nursed my babies, cuddled them as toddlers, and taught two of them from kindergarten to high school—at home. My circle of family and friends was small, and few people outside of that circle even knew I wrote.

My debut novel sold out within two weeks of being published, and the popularity of the series continued to grow until my third book hit the *New York Times* bestseller list. To celebrate, my family and I went out to eat at a really nice restaurant. The news was fun, but I was glad that the impact seemed nominal.

When I woke the next day, I began to feel a shift. I'd gone to bed the same woman and woke with…tangible respect. It felt truly odd. I hadn't changed, but e-mails and phone messages were waiting. People, many of whom had known me for years, suddenly wanted me to come speak at their book clubs, women's functions, libraries, and bookstores. I was struck by the oddity of it. Did I know a lot more today than yesterday? Was I more qualified today?

I had no more value after I became an author than when I was in my home tending to runny noses, little bumps and bruises, and laboring over hard-fought-for school lessons my children would never remember learning (even though the skill became a part of them). Our value can't be wrapped inside what others think or we think, because that is too dependent on this ever-shifting world. The value God places on us makes us more than we think we are, even on our hardest days, weeks, or years.

HOPE

Therefore being justified by faith, we have
peace with God through our Lord Jesus
Christ: By whom also we have access by faith
into this grace wherein we stand, and rejoice
in hope of the glory of God.

—ROMANS 5:1–2

From Cindy

When I came to Christ in my early twenties, the one characteristic of who
He is that changed everything about my life was *hope*. It seemed to create
its own sense of thankfulness and well-being.

At first, thinking on hopeful things didn't come naturally for me. A
hopeful thought would skitter through my mind so fast I couldn't catch
it. It seemed to take about five minutes to recall the hopeful thought, but
I chased it down. And every time it slipped away, I chased it down again.

A hopeful thought would come to me, and negative ones would
stomp all over it, trying to assure me that gloomy thinking was realistic
and hope was a liar. I had to purposefully latch on to hope. I had to protect hope, standing firm against pessimism over and over again—for
days, months, and years.

God's love, in whatever form it shows itself, wants to give us hope.

Whenever welcomed and protected, hope joins the rhythm of our
daily life, and it whispers encouragement morning, noon, and night—
through every season.

I know from my own walk that if we'll hang on to hope, it will grow stronger than despair. Hope in who He is. Hope in who we can be. Hope for our loved ones' futures.

Hope sees what cannot be seen with human eyes. It feels what we cannot touch with our hands. And it accomplishes what cannot be possible.

From Miriam

Giving my fingers a break from the pricking needle, I sat back and admired the beautiful quilt stretched out before me. The colorful fabric pieces formed a perfect Shining Lone Star pattern. A dozen or more ladies sat around the quilt frame, stitching away as we all got better acquainted.

For years the Cumberland Valley Relief Center in Chambersburg, Pennsylvania, in cooperation with the Mennonite Central Committee, has opened its doors to many different church groups, allowing them to come together to volunteer their time for a variety of relief projects. There is a job for everyone: some quilt or knot comforters, others weave rugs or make homemade soap, and still others prepare health kits, AIDS kits, newborn-care kits, and school kits—all to be shipped to people in need.

We also help with the Mennonite Central Committee's meat-canning ministry, which has been providing food to hungry people for the past sixty-two years. Every year people in approximately thirty-eight locations across the United States and Canada can high-quality meats to ship to at least twenty-two countries. These shipments, along with other kinds of material aid, provide significant help for the poor.

When the traveling cannery comes to the Chambersburg area for a week's worth of canning, the churches come together. Fresh boneless turkey thighs are cut and canned. The cans are washed, labeled, and packed for shipment. By the end of the week, forty-eight thousand pounds of meat have been packaged in 26,880 cans. The whole process is under inspection, and all volunteers are required to wear white caps and aprons or coats.

As I stood at the door of the cutting room, observing the assembly line with everyone dressed in white, I envisioned a bit of heaven on earth—people of diverse backgrounds from different church groups with varied lifestyles all coming together…working side by side for the sake of others…bringing them hope and encouragement…in honor of the same God.

Kitchen Tables

Part 1

Better is a dry morsel, and quietness there-
with, than an house full of sacrifices with
strife.

—Proverbs 17:1

From Cindy

When our two older boys were in high school, they joined numerous extracurricular activities. My husband and I had known the busy teen years would shift how we handled our days, and we were ready to roll with the punches. But our five-year-old was caught off guard.

One evening I prepared a meal, set it on the table, and called our youngest to the table. The house was empty except for the two of us. His teenage brothers were at marching band practice, and Dad was still at work. Tyler came to the kitchen, took his plate off the table, and moved it to the island. "Lunch again, Mom?"

"No, this is dinner."

He frowned and shook his head. "It's not a real dinnertime unless everyone is here to sit at the table."

"But you said you were hungry. And your brothers and dad won't be home for another two hours."

"I'm not hungry for food as much as I wanted us to have dinner together." He pushed the plate back. "Can I just have an apple?"

I knew what he meant. I felt the same way.

Is it possible that when God created humans to need food, part of the plan had nothing to do with meeting physical needs? Newborns can't feed themselves, so their first connection to Mom and Dad is warm, tasty milk filling their empty bellies while the parents snuggle with them, making eye contact, cooing or singing. Putting a high priority on that bonding time is good seed for future relationships and self-esteem.

Sometimes I wonder how emotionally distant we could become if our physical bodies didn't require sustenance. Fortunately, adults eat two or three times a day, so we have numerous opportunities to come together and emotionally connect with those we share a life with.

From Miriam

Every year we hold an Amish school sale, auctioning off homemade items to English and Amish alike, to raise funds for the local school. To reward those who organize and survive the busy auction, we hold a lobster supper. Our friends from Massachusetts, Chuck and Carolyn, have been faithfully attending the sale and bringing fresh lobsters for the past eight years. We add steaks, baked potatoes, a salad, and some fresh fruit, and it turns out to be quite a feast.

The evening of the thirty-first annual auction, a weary group gathered around my dining room table, ready to relax and unwind. At the last minute my husband and I decided to add a few more leaves to extend the table. While we pulled on both ends at once, the runners underneath gave way. My table broke in half and crashed to the floor, spilling platters of food and cups of melted butter everywhere. One guest went sliding across the floor, nearly falling in a puddle of butter.

I just stood there, watching the chaotic scene around me, too stunned and embarrassed to move. Finally getting down on all fours to retrieve a runaway potato, I came face to face with my husband, who was going after the lobster. Daniel looked at me and said, "Monday morning you go to Zimmerman's Furniture and buy a new table."

Suddenly my humiliation turned to excitement. My old table had been giving me grief for a long time, and the prospect of owning a new one was thrilling.

The right word spoken at the right moment can turn a negative situation into a positive one. When our perspective of an event changes, our attitudes change as well, even if the circumstances remain the same. After the table had been temporarily put back together and I was helping my guests find their places again, I felt blessed for our time around the table. Even a broken one. Even in the midst of all the chaos. Somehow those pieces of wood had managed to knit us all together.

The Waiting Game

But let patience have her perfect work,
that ye may be perfect and entire, wanting
nothing.

—James 1:4

From Amanda (Miriam's daughter)

The week before Christmas, snow fell outside, and the windows creaked and groaned from the wind. Inside, the fireplace shed a warm glow across the floor and set to shimmering the shiny wrapping paper on the many gifts stacked beside me. I had just finished wrapping the last one and added a small green bow.

As I looked at all the packages, my eye caught a middle-sized one wrapped in blue paper. Mom had wrapped it, and I knew it was mine. Suddenly I could hardly wait for Christmas! I eagerly anticipated the day when my whole family would get together to exchange gifts, sing holiday songs, and enjoy family fellowship.

Clasping my hands in front of me, I envisioned my siblings' smiling faces as they peeled back the last of the paper, revealing their gifts inside. Excitement surged through me at the thought of my own blue box.

Then I thought about Christmas being Jesus's birthday. There I was, surrounded by packages, bags, and boxes full of beautiful and useful items, but none were addressed to Him.

I bowed my head and breathed, *What can I give You for Christmas, Lord?*

In a whisper as quiet as the falling snow, I heard Him say, *Your heart.*

From Cindy

My dad didn't believe in bribing his children into good behavior. We were to tell the truth, work hard, and keep our mouths shut at all the appropriate times simply because those were the right things to do. And with a no-nonsense dad like mine, we did.

The only time he seemed to have no qualms about offering incentives was during vacations.

At least once each year, we traveled from Maryland to Big Mama and Big Daddy's home in Glencoe, Alabama. If we four kids could make it to a key spot of the sixteen-hour trip without a break, he'd stop at a specific roadside stand and buy each of us one thing we wanted. The budget was one dollar per person, but Dad would cover the tax. He even allowed items slightly over a dollar.

We each got the same treat every time. My sister wanted orange slices. My oldest brother wanted saltwater taffy. My other brother wanted a pecan roll. And I wanted one of those adjustable rings.

After traveling for what seemed like forever, I'd see him look at his watch, then in the rearview mirror. "We've got about two more hours. How's it going back there?"

Oh how I could have used a restroom, a cup of water, and a few moments to stretch my legs. But I'd say, "I'm good. Do you think they'll have the deep blue turquoise ones this time?"

He'd smile. "I don't see why not."

Once we stopped and after we all hurried to the restroom and back, Dad would stand beside me at the jewelry stand and help me pick out the ring I'd been dreaming of for a month. I loved that he helped me choose. It sealed my sense of victory, and the man behind the counter treated me with respect rather than urging me to hurry up.

Many years later I realized that Dad had figured out ahead of time just how long I, as the youngest, could comfortably go between bathroom breaks. Then he added a little time. That way he could get as far as possible, and I could feel victorious with the ring on my finger.

Those experiences taught me the power of ignoring my body's impulses in order to attain a higher goal. I learned that I could meet a challenge and that others could benefit from my restraint. I also discovered that the sweetest part of any victory is the sense of winning against one's own self. And that hard times go by much more quickly when hope is calling.

That was a lot to learn when all my dad wanted was to get to the destination as quickly as possible while keeping the mood light during the long trip. What lessons can your children learn if you plan something that requires them to be responsible for part of the success?

TIMELESS
BEGINNINGS

WEDDINGS AND GIFTS

Whenever Miriam talks about an upcoming wedding, I know from the joy I see on her face or hear in her voice that marriage is a time of great celebration for the Amish. A wedding is a sign that a man and woman have carefully considered their future and have chosen to join the faith, marry, and raise a family in the same way they were raised. They're ready to leave the carefree days of youth behind and take on the adult responsibilities of helping the community remain strong.

But many outside the Amish community wonder how couples find each other. Do they date? Do they have to find someone within their district? within their faith?

To some extent it begins with *rumschpringe* (pronounced *room-shpring'-uh*), the Pennsylvania Dutch word for "running around." Rumschpringe provides a bridge between childhood and adulthood by giving Amish young people extra freedoms and the opportunity to decide if they're going to join the faith and also to find a spouse. It usually begins around sixteen years old, and although there isn't an exact time for it to end, parents encourage their children to make a decision about the Amish faith by their early twenties.

But good parenting doesn't end when young people enter their rumschpringe. I was staying with an Old Order Amish friend a few years ago when an Amish holiday rolled around. Everyone had the day off, and the parents did their best to provide an outlet for the teens to get together and have fun among plenty of chaperones. The parents chipped in and bought pizza and drinks. Since it was pouring rain, they set up volleyball nets inside a warehouse-type building.

This is typical of the Old Order Amish. The parents want to offer freedom and fun for their young people as well as a safe, controlled environment. One provision the adults make for the young people is to schedule singings every Sunday night at an adult's home or barn, with a church leader or parent facilitating. The boys sit on one side of a long table, and the girls sit on the other. A church leader or one of the older singles usually begins the song—often an upbeat worship song from the German hymnal—and others will join in. Occasionally someone will sing a song that he or she composed, and others will sing along as they learn the tune and lyrics. After the singing the young men and women socialize over desserts and cold beverages in hot weather and hot beverages in cold weather.

The young people may attend singings in any district they wish, and sometimes adults will organize a singing for an entire region. Parents also host a lot of other youth gatherings: volleyball games, cookouts, bonfires, all with plenty of desserts and beverages. In the winter several parents may work together to host several districts of youth at one of their homes and play games such as Dutch Blitz, Ping-Pong, or a fast-paced card game that is sure to rattle the windows with laughs and howls.

When an Amish couple falls in love, they have a few obstacles to overcome before they can marry. Each must join the faith if they have not done so already. And to do this, they must go through several months of instruction classes on church Sundays, starting in late spring. The bishop or a church leader teaches these classes, and he covers the principles, doctrines, and scriptures that help the young person understand the commitment he or she is making to Christ, the community, and the Amish way of life.

A couple is officially engaged when they announce it to family or friends, but the next obstacle is waiting for the wedding season, in autumn. Most become engaged in the spring so they have time to prepare for a wedding in the fall. In early autumn the groom will go to the bishop and seek his blessing. Even though the parents know about the couple's plans by this point, the groom will also ask the girl's father for his approval and blessing.

The couple will then be "published," which means that the bishop or a minister will announce it during a church service, and then someone within the community will place their names and the date of their wedding in an Amish newspaper—either *The Budget* or *Die Botschaft*, which means "the message." A couple is usually published in late October.

Although many within the community help prepare for the wedding, most of the responsibility falls on the bride and her family. Since the Amish don't have church buildings, weddings most often take place on property belonging to the bride's parents. If the parents can't accommodate the guests, the wedding may take place at the home of a close relative.

Using the same color fabric, the bride and her mother make dresses for the bride and all the women and girls in her immediate family. The groom's mother makes matching dresses for the women in her family. Both mothers make white shirts and, if necessary, black suits for the men. The bride's mother provides two meals on the day of the wedding: a dinner and a supper. But the family has already spent a lot of time preparing for this day, having planted lots of extra vegetables to serve on the wedding day and to stock the new couple's pantry with plenty of canned goods.

The traditional Amish wedding ceremony doesn't have flowers, but the groom usually sends a bouquet of roses to his fiancée's home the morning of the wedding.

Because singing is such an integral part of the couple's meeting and courting, the Amish enjoy long periods of group singing on the day of the wedding. They usually sing German wedding songs as well as a few Amish favorites of the bride and groom.

Amish couples don't register for gifts at stores, as many non-Amish brides do, and there is no bridal shower. Instead, the Amish have two main ways to give gifts: at the wedding ceremony or when the couple visits the homes of family and friends sometime after the ceremony.

Gifts may include nonelectric kitchenware, quilts, canned goods, towels, an outdoor gas grill, a porch swing, a drying rack for clothes, garden or shop tools, or even an express wagon (much like our children's wagons, only larger and nicer with rubber tires and removable racks). They're great for walking a load of items to a neighbor's house. When Miriam's oldest son married, she gave the young couple several gifts, but the one I found the most fascinating was a feed scoop. She filled it with a homemade trail mix that looked like horse feed. After the big meal was over and the singing began, Miriam set the scoop on a table. The young people had a great time passing it around and taking a handful of "horse feed."

Following the wedding, the bride and groom spend a day or two helping to clean up. After accommodating from two hundred to five hundred people in an Amish home, the host has loads of kitchen towels, cloth napkins, and tablecloths for the women to wash in the wringer washer and hang on the line—not to mention all the clothes that became dirty or stained during the daylong celebration. Most of the wedding guests come from within the district or nearby districts. Those who arrive by train or hired driver will often stay overnight with friends or relatives who live in the area.

The men have benches and tables to remove from the house and take to wherever church will be held the next Sunday. Furniture also has to be moved back in place from its storage area, which is often a spare bedroom or a barn.

The Amish handle this workload as they handle all of life. Everyone pitches in: the bride and her siblings, aunts, uncles, and cousins as well as close friends of the family (who will themselves need help when they have a wedding in their home). The Amish may not know the saying "Pay it forward," but they live the lifestyle.

From Miriam

This recipe is used for weddings. It's one of the candy dishes passed around during the daylong celebration.

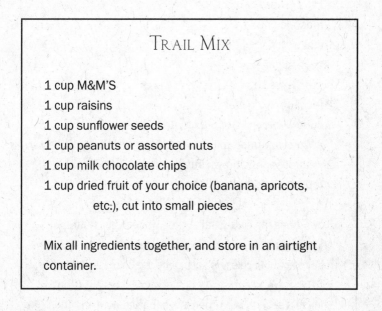

TRAIL MIX

1 cup M&M'S
1 cup raisins
1 cup sunflower seeds
1 cup peanuts or assorted nuts
1 cup milk chocolate chips
1 cup dried fruit of your choice (banana, apricots,
        etc.), cut into small pieces

Mix all ingredients together, and store in an airtight container.

From Cindy

My Old Order Amish friend Rachel made an entire wedding meal for me during one of my visits. She invited some mutual friends, and we had a marvelous time! The food and fellowship were outstanding, but I've yet to get comfortable with her sacrifice of time. Of all the foods she'd prepared as part of the typical Amish wedding feast, I saw one I hadn't expected to like—cooked celery. I like celery, but I'd never eaten it cooked. It was so good I had a second helping. Rachel's mother even prepared a bowl of it for me to take back to Miriam's so I could have more at lunch the next day.

COOKED CELERY FOR SIX

2 quarts celery, cut into bite-size pieces (Note: 1$\frac{1}{2}$ to 2 stalks of celery equal two quarts, and a stalk consists of approximately a dozen individual ribs.)

1 teaspoon salt

1 cup water

$\frac{1}{2}$ cup sugar

butter, the size of a walnut

2 teaspoons vinegar

2 cups whole milk, approximately

$\frac{1}{2}$ cup evaporated milk

2$\frac{1}{2}$ tablespoons brown sugar

2 tablespoons flour

Slowly bring the celery, salt, water, white sugar, butter, and vinegar to a low boil. Cook ingredients for about 10 minutes or until celery is soft. Once the celery is soft, cover with whole milk, and slowly heat to almost boiling. (Don't bring to a second boil.) Then in a separate bowl, mix the evaporated milk, brown sugar, and flour until the mixture is smooth, and slowly add it to the rest of the ingredients. Stir until thoroughly heated, and serve it warm.

Kitchen Tables

Part 2

Thy wife shall be as a fruitful vine by the
sides of thine house: thy children like olive
plants round about thy table.

—Psalm 128:3

From Cindy

Adding a baby to a family is not new upon this earth. It's been a regular occurrence since Adam and Eve had their first child. Yet each newborn is a fresh start, not just for the infant, but also for the family.

Usually by six months the little one is sitting in a highchair at the family table. A lot of growing up takes place at the kitchen table. Here weary, hungry bodies are refreshed. Manners are learned. Laughter is heard. Tears are spilled as the weight of the day is shared with those around us. Lessons are taught. Fears are conveyed. Confidence is built.

A kitchen table holds far more than bowls, plates, and platters. Even now, with my youngest almost grown, I hear laughter at the table...often when my adult children recall all the unsuccessful new recipes I set before them during their childhood. And I hear lively discussions as we each want the others to see some aspect of life from a different perspective—because learning about life at the table is something we should never outgrow.

From Miriam

On Monday morning I stood at the kitchen table looking at the piece of furniture I was about to replace. I ran my hand over the top, feeling all the dents and scratches from years gone by, gazing at the splatters of tole paint left behind from countless crafts. Each mark had a story.

A lot had taken place around this table in the past twenty-five years. I served my first meals to my new husband here. After our fourth child arrived, we added a leaf. This was where we'd celebrated all their birthdays and taught them to pray at mealtime.

Many Thanksgiving, Easter, and Christmas dinners had been shared as we gathered around this table. We added yet another leaf when we welcomed our two daughters-in-law, and we extended the table again recently to make room for our dear grandchildren.

This is where we as a family have gathered not only to take in food to nourish our bodies but to partake of spiritual food for our souls as we have celebrated life, God's love, and our love for Him and for one another. Here we have shared our disappointments and heartaches.

The more I thought about it, the idea of a new table became less appealing. In spite of its wobbly ways, I held off making that trip to Zimmerman's.

Spring planting gave way to summer chores and activities. Soon we were into the fall harvest, with the holidays just around the corner. My unsteady old table had to be replaced before the next huge family gathering.

But when my good English friend Katrine offered to help refinish the old table, I eagerly agreed. We sanded for days, removing the old finish, the dents, and the scratches. We took the extension runners apart and sanded each one smooth, then securely reattached them. Then came the staining and coats of polyurethane. My beat-up old table was transformed into a beautiful heirloom.

On Thanksgiving Day, as my family gathered around my "new" table, I felt extremely grateful for my friend's help as she'd selflessly sacrificed her time, skill, and effort. I felt truly blessed by her friendship, and I was thrilled to be able to restore and strengthen the most important piece of furniture in my home.

In much the same way, when we give our hearts to God, we change from the old to the new. He sands down the rough selves, transforming us into new selves by grace, with faith. As 2 Corinthians 5:17 says, "Therefore if any man be in Christ, he is a new creature: old things are passed away; behold, all things are become new."

UNDERESTIMATED POWER

Therefore I say unto you, what things soever
ye desire, when ye pray, believe that ye receive
them, and ye shall have them.

—MARK 11:24

From Cindy

Some of my favorite childhood memories are wrapped around special family times. And I'm not talking about just when we were on vacation or having a birthday party but during those occasions when each family member stepped out of the busyness of his or her world and truly connected with those who shared the same home.

From the time I was eight until I entered high school, my family lived in various parts of rural Maryland. In one place we lost electricity to our home fairly often. We were well equipped to deal with the outages—a potbelly stove for cold weather, plenty of goods my mother had canned from her garden, and several kerosene lamps. So we had warmth, food, and light. What more could a family need?

Games! Fast-paced, easy ones, where the goal is laughter, not winning.

During those times when the television was as dark as the night, we'd clear the kitchen table, set a lantern on it, and start a board game. Not having electricity caused everyone naturally to shift his or her normal routine.

For me, what was most fun about those evenings was having my parents' undivided attention. Parents are often so busy being parents that their children don't get to see their true personalities—the one that shows up when Mom goes out with her girlfriends or when Dad and his co-workers eat lunch together at a restaurant.

Game night, which only occurred when the electricity went out, helped shape my thoughts about my family. It gave me a glimpse into my mom's carefree side and my dad's sharp wit, which had us roaring with laughter. Temporarily being without electricity was an inconvenience to my parents, who had work to do. But it radiated a light inside my heart that has lasted a lifetime.

The Old Order Amish live without electricity all the time.

Do I want to live the way they do? With much respect to them, I say, "No, thank you."

Do the Amish want to live as we do? With much respect to Englisch-ers, the Amish I know say, "No, thank you."

We'd each have to give up things we cherish. I'd have to alter much of the life I've always known, and while I was at it, I would likely be alter-ing the lives of my family for future generations.

But there are common denominators in the two traditions—like our determination to protect our families and keep them a priority. And our belief in the power of love, which doesn't originate with any particular tradition—not Amish or Englischer—but comes from the love God has for us. "Eye hath not seen, nor ear heard, neither have entered into the heart of man, the things which God hath prepared for them that love him" (1 Corinthians 2:9).

From Miriam

Physically, I was cleaning walls, windows, cupboards, and floors. Men-tally, I was planning menus for the two meals to be held in our home the next day. The first meal would follow the church service in our home and feed everyone who attended. The Amish hold church services in people's homes every other week, rotating the responsibility for hosting the service and the meal afterward. The second meal of the day was for close friends and extended family. The ladies all bring loaves of homemade bread and desserts to share, which is a big help. But the main course is the responsibility of the host family, which this week was me.

Going over the list in my head, I felt confident that I had all I needed for lunch: bread, ham, cheese spread, peanut butter, pickles, red beets, pies, and coffee—enough to feed the whole congregation of approximately 110 people.

Only our families and a few close friends would stay for the evening meal. I planned to serve meat loaf, mashed potatoes, peas, a salad, and noodles for that one. Dessert would be cakes, pies, pudding, and fresh fruit for the health conscious, but I'd forgotten to buy fruit. Several of the folks couldn't eat much of anything except fruit, so I started to panic. Going to town was out of the question, as I'd already gone twice that week. A third trip would require arranging for a driver, which was somewhat costly, assuming I could find one on such short notice. The only store close enough to reach by horse and buggy had already closed for the day.

Scolding myself for being so scatterbrained, I breathed a quick prayer. *Lord, tomorrow is Your day, and this is Your church.* Knowing I couldn't do anything about the problem, I focused on moving furniture out and benches in as we set up for church.

About an hour later I heard a car in the driveway. Pulling back the curtain to see who it was, I gasped in disbelief. An English friend was coming up the walk, carrying a huge fruit basket! I choked up, both surprised and ashamed—ashamed that I was so surprised at my answered prayer.

It had seemed like too small a thing to bring before the Lord. But He had heard and He cared, and I was reminded never to underestimate the power of prayer...even for seemingly insignificant requests.

We serve certain foods at every after-church meal. The peanut butter spread is a favorite.

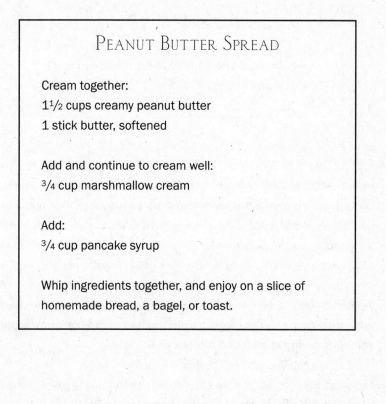

Peanut Butter Spread

Cream together:
1½ cups creamy peanut butter
1 stick butter, softened

Add and continue to cream well:
¾ cup marshmallow cream

Add:
¾ cup pancake syrup

Whip ingredients together, and enjoy on a slice of homemade bread, a bagel, or toast.

Patience Is Waiting Without Anger

And let us not be weary in well doing: for in
due season we shall reap, if we faint not.

—Galatians 6:9

From Miriam

In the spring of 1971, when the first families from Lancaster County, Pennsylvania, bought farms and settled in the picturesque valley in Franklin County, Pennsylvania, lots of issues needed to be worked out. Since the Amish hold their church services in people's homes, a place to worship was no problem. But schooling the children was. They had only a few scholars (schoolchildren) in their midst, so sending the kids to the local Mennonite school seemed the best solution. But it was ten miles away, which is quite a distance when one needs to hitch a horse to a buggy and travel twenty miles round trip twice daily.

As time went on, more families moved into the area. The church grew, and another Amish congregation was established. They now had enough children and teachers to start their own school.

A vacant brick building, which had been used as a school by the English years ago, was an ideal place for a one-room school. But the owner was not interested in selling or even renting it. So the Amish children continued attending the Mennonite school ten miles away.

Several years later an English neighbor lost his barn because of an electrical fire. It was a beautiful old barn and had been in the family for generations. Sadly, it burned down to the stone foundation.

As the sun rose the next morning, a smoky haze enveloped the old homestead. Neighbors came from all directions with tools and plenty of ambition. The cleanup went swiftly, and plans were made to rebuild.

Just outside of town stood another old barn, which the owner wanted torn down and removed from his property. Its dimensions fit the foundation of the burned barn perfectly. So arrangements were made to tear down, transplant, and rebuild.

On the day of the barn raising, three busloads of Amish men from Lancaster County came to help, and by sundown a recycled barn stood on its adopted foundation.

Days after the barn raising, one of the Amish school board members was milking his cows in the evening when the owner of the old brick schoolhouse stopped by. With tears streaming down his weathered face, he walked up to the dairy farmer and said, "I want the Amish to have my brick schoolhouse as my way of thanking everyone for what they did for my brother in replacing his barn. You see, I grew up on that farm."

The farmer bowed his head in humble gratitude, with tears in his own eyes, and then he shook hands with the English fellow. Feeling unworthy of such a great gift, he thanked God for the friendship, acceptance, and unity of their new community.

The man's earlier decision not to sell the schoolhouse had been a disappointing one. As the parents and scholars rose extra early to travel to the Mennonite school and arrived back home late each school day, I'm sure there were some frustrations. Yet when the man's barn burned, I witnessed my community respond to him according to the Golden Rule (see Matthew 7:12). And that situation planted seeds of understanding in me: following God's principles always yields a good crop. Eventually.

From Cindy

Tommy and I have been blessed with two daughters-in-law. One is a first-generation American who moved here from India at the age of eight years old. She and our oldest son, Justin, met while attending the Medical

College of Georgia. At first he found her intelligent, beautiful, and annoying. Her opinions about life were every bit as strong as his, and most were different. He began a study group and invited anyone from class who was interested in attending. She came. Over the next few months, they discovered that they agreed on much more than they disagreed on. As opportunities arose, he sprinkled into conversations his strong belief in God the Father, Son, and Holy Spirit. She became a believer, and their interest in each other grew.

But if they pursued a romantic relationship, acceptance from her relatives wouldn't come easily. In the Indian culture, children are to choose a spouse from their community with strong guidance from their parents. Starting a relationship based on attraction or love is forbidden.

So they had to be patient yet unyielding. Gentle yet adamant. With each step they took, they fell deeper in love, clinging to the hope that they could win her family's approval.

Since his infancy I had prayed regularly for Justin to find the right spouse. I couldn't assume she was the wrong one just because her parents had deep concerns or because she'd been raised in the Hindu religion. But I understood and respected her family's position; her parents are good and loving, and they only wanted to do what they believed was right.

Justin and Shweta sought the wisdom and counsel of their pastor and continued to be patient, but when they knew the time was right, they set a wedding date. The time that followed was tremendously stressful for everyone and often filled with tears.

But much to our joy and as a testimony to her parents' fervent love, they came to the wedding.

FINDING PEACE

To every thing there is a season, and a time
to every purpose under the heaven.

—ECCLESIASTES 3:1

From Cindy

In the first photo of me as a toddler, I'm holding a damp washcloth in my hand, scrubbing my older brother's face. In the next photo, I'm using that same rag to dust the furniture. I'm sure I was mimicking what I'd seen my mother do—dust furniture and wash children's faces—although I'm confident she didn't use the same rag for both.

Cleanliness was important to my mom—especially for hands and faces—before my brothers, sister, and I came to the kitchen table. My mom often sent us back to the bathroom to "try again." Mark, a true outdoorsman and bicycle mechanic from an early age, had the hardest time passing inspection. One day when my mom told him his hands were still dirty, he studied them, held them up to her again, and said, "Mom, I think it's your eyeballs that are dirty. Have you tried washing them?"

She burst into laughter, agreed that maybe he was right, and let him take a seat at the table. It seemed to me that she was never as picky about clean hands after that.

Whenever I have a negative opinion about something a person put effort into, I ask myself if my eyeballs need washing. Am I being too picky? Is the problem how I'm viewing the situation? If people in your life are having a difficult time passing your inspection, it's possible that your eyeballs need washing.

Finding peace with our imperfect world and its imperfect people isn't always easy, but if we don't find a way to let go of our stringent ideals of how things should be, we'll never be free to enjoy the greatest gifts life gives us.

From Miriam

One crisp, breezy November morning, I stepped out the back door of my home and headed toward the clothesline, carrying a basket loaded with clean, wet clothes. For weeks I had sewn feverishly—new white shirts and black pants for my husband and five sons, and traditional matching dresses for my daughter and myself—in preparation for my second son's wedding. The wedding had taken place the day before, and the celebration had been even more than I'd hoped for.

As I hung the white shirts on the clothesline, a lump formed in my throat. I have always counted my blessings by how many Sunday shirts I had to wash and hang out after a church day. If I had six, that meant my whole family had attended church the day before. Any fewer probably meant that one of the teenage boys had not attended, which always brought heartache.

So there I was with a shirt missing. With mixed emotions I choked back the tears. My son was no longer mine. As thrilled as I was for him, I hurt.

My fingers ached with the cold by the time I hung up the last shirt, grabbed the clothesbasket, and trudged inside. As I stood by the wood-burning cookstove, warming my hands, I looked out the window and across the field. In the distance I saw a white shirt hanging on a neighbor's clothesline, and it reminded me that my son's shirt wasn't missing. It was simply on someone else's clothesline—his wife's. All his hopes for his future and his family's future hung in the same crisp November air.

I had not lost a son. His life was no longer under my roof, but it was in the same place I'd put it when he was born: in the hands of God.

New Day

Blessed be God, even the Father of our Lord
Jesus Christ, the Father of mercies, and the
God of all comfort.

—2 Corinthians 1:3

From Miriam

In the play yard of our one-room schoolhouse, snowballs flew by me, and occasionally one hit its mark. I fired my own snowballs in return. The weather had turned warmer, but the melting snow was perfect for a snowball battle.

It was my last day of school before my family moved to a new Amish community forty miles away, and I knew I'd miss all my friends. Giggles, laughter, and yelps abounded as we made the most of the last half hour of recess.

Suddenly the noise hushed, and all my schoolmates looked at me. Someone launched a snowball in my direction. Then a few more joined in. Soon the whole school was throwing snowballs at me. I was their only target.

At first I laughed with them. But as the snowballs whizzed faster, they hit me harder, stinging me. I darted from one snow fort to the next—the ones we'd been building for many days during recess—dodging the frozen missiles the best I could.

I knew this was all in fun, but for me it wasn't fun anymore. I'd never felt so scared and alone. Just when I was about to give in to the tears that threatened to spill down my cheeks, I felt someone at my side. It was my friend Susie, and she was dodging the balls with me. She could have stayed on the other side, but she chose to come alongside me and help me find shelter.

As I left school that day, I knew I'd miss Susie the most, and I wished I could take her with me to the new school. But remembering her, our friendship, and her bravery would help me face the new beginnings that lay before me.

From Cindy

No other house was in sight as I stood outside my home with my brother, waiting for the bus to arrive for the first day at our new schools. Unlike our home in the suburbs of DC, the old farm we'd bought that summer didn't have a neighbor within sight. All the folks who lived around here knew each other, because my dad said most of the families were living on dairy farms that had once belonged to their parents and their parents before them. We, on the other hand, were outsiders. That had seemed sort of cool when we first arrived. Now I felt awkward and lonely.

The bus pulled up, and I boarded with my brother. He wasn't going to the same school, but he'd be with me until the bus stopped at my elementary school. I sat beside him, and we rode in silence as the huge vehicle went down one long, narrow road after another until I lost all sense of direction.

The other seats filled with strangers who kept looking at us and whispering.

Finally the bus stopped at a school, and my brother nudged me and whispered, "This is it. Get out." When I looked up at him with wide eyes, he added, "You'll be fine."

At least half of the riders got off the bus with me. Most were boys, who looked at me funny, but no one said a word.

I overheard that the fourth-grade class was on the second floor, so I navigated up stairwells and down unfamiliar hallways until I found my room. I was barely inside when someone said, "There she is." Before I took two more steps, I was surrounded by a group of frowning boys.

"What's your name?" one asked.

I told him.

"What kind of last name is that?" The boy wrinkled his nose, looking me dead in the eyes.

"The only one I got." An unfamiliar knot formed in my stomach. I'd been to new schools before, but this one seemed awfully unfriendly.

A girl with a kind face, old-fashioned clothes, and a small bonnet covering her head stood at the outer edge of the group of boys, watching. My first thought was that the school was going to have a play about pilgrims. But it seemed odd to have a play on the first day of school.

A boy moved his head, blocking my view of the girl. "Frank said you ride on his bus."

I wondered who Frank was.

"He said your dad ain't a farmer. Everybody around here owns or works a dairy farm."

I shrugged. "My dad works in DC and drives back and forth."

"DC?" the boy mocked.

The squeals of laughter made the teacher glance up from his desk. "Settle down. You have three minutes before you need to take your seats. Make sure you have pencil and paper ready."

The boy lowered his voice and moved in closer. "So why'd your dad buy all that land with barns and fences if he don't intend to farm?"

"It's a hobby farm…I think."

The whispery scoffs spoke louder than the boys dared to. "Every one of us has been up since four this morning doing chores. Farming ain't no hobby."

The girl with the bonnet pressed forward, and the group parted, much as I'd imagined the Red Sea parting for the Israelites. "I think you guys are coming on a bit strong, no?"

"We're just asking questions."

"Would your mother want you talking to her that way?" The girl's voice was soft, as if cooing to an infant rather than standing up to a bunch of rowdy kids. A couple of the boys moved to their desks and sat down. Others asked a few more mocking questions, and the girl repeated herself, never raising her voice: "Would your mother want you talking to her that way?" She took me by the hand and led me to the back of the room, where it was quiet. The boys kept a wary eye on us as they walked to their desks.

"They don't mean to sound so rude." She slowly lifted her eyes to mine. "That's what my mom says anyway."

I was struck by the kindness in her eyes, the oddity of her speech patterns, and how smart she was.

She introduced herself as Luann. I later learned that her bonnet was a prayer Kapp and that she was an Amish Mennonite. Her father wasn't a dairy farmer either. So she was used to being treated as different and odd, and she seemed perfectly comfortable not fitting in with those around her.

I learned a lot that day about being soft-spoken but not silent, about responding calmly and yet saying all that needs to be said. And I learned that it takes only one person to make a new beginning feel hopeful.

WORK ETHIC

Study to be quiet, and to do your own
business, and to work with your own hands,
as we commanded you.

—1 THESSALONIANS 4:11

From Miriam

As I think back on my childhood years, I remember the aromas of baking day—breads, cakes, shoofly pies, fruit pies, cinnamon rolls, cookies, and whoopie pies. I often worked side by side with my mother and my four sisters as each week we baked goods, mostly to sell from our roadside stand in the front yard.

Mother's hands were constantly busy. Besides raising a family, she always had an occupation in the home to help make ends meet. I spent hours playing with the children she baby-sat, picking strawberries with her, and plucking the feathers of chickens that we butchered to sell.

But what stands out most in my mind is her love for her work. Whether baking, sewing, quilting, gardening, or "playing" in her flower beds, she truly enjoyed working and still does. At seventy years old, she has raised seven children and had double knee replacements yet still runs the bake shop by herself.

As a young girl, I lacked the ambition my mother has. I'd avoid work wherever and whenever possible. But somewhere along the line, my mother managed to instill a work ethic in me—one I hope to pass on to the next generation.

I see my mother in myself when I feel a sense of satisfaction in a job accomplished. I also see a younger version of myself in my children when their motivation doesn't match mine.

I'm sure it took discipline for my mother to become such a hard worker, and I have to admit that challenge continues for me as well as for my younger children. But it encourages me to see that my adult children have become quite industrious, and they are now teaching their own families to love work and to value accomplishing a goal.

From Cindy

I remember my mom dripping with perspiration as she picked blackberries and canned them in summer. I can still smell the rich soil as she planted her large vegetable garden in spring. And I remember how tan her hands were from hanging laundry on the line all year round. Whether we lived on a small farm in the Northeast or in rural Alabama or a few miles outside of Washington DC, Mom worked diligently and had specific goals for every season.

My dad left for work before daylight and often arrived home after dark, even in the summer months. He had projects mapped out for every weekend—painting a clapboard house; wallpapering a kitchen; building a barn, shed, or garage; or using the rototiller on a piece of ground that had never been tilled before.

Because he and Mom bought houses cheap, fixed them up, and sold them for a profit, their idea of home didn't fit the image I longed for—the one I saw on television or read about in books.

Neither Mom nor Dad graduated from high school, and both had grown up very poor.

Every year when school began, my mom took me shopping and bought me two or three outfits to go with my mostly homemade clothes. By the time I was in middle school, I hated the clothes she'd sewn for me on her machine and often tried to talk her into buying me more clothes.

One afternoon she was at her sewing machine, which fit into a corner next to her bed. I heard the familiar whirring sound, and then I heard her gasp, "Oh no!"

I went to see what was up. She was sitting at her machine with a pair of my dad's pants.

"Mom?"

Her eyes were filled with tears. "I can't patch them again. They're too threadbare." She wiggled a finger through the gaping hole.

"Buy him another pair."

She shook her head. "I can't, but he has to have at least two pairs of pants—one to wash, one to wear."

Two pairs? Why would my dad have only two pairs of pants? I went to their closet and opened it. There were four shirts and a jacket but no pants. Realization trickled in as I studied the room. A freshly mended sheet lay neatly folded in the stack of items she'd been repairing. I'd teased her and Dad the night before about the ridiculousness of repairing sheets time and again. They'd laughed with me.

Suddenly I saw their life differently. She didn't sew clothes, pick blackberries, tend gardens, and can foods because it brought her pleasure—although doing those things always seemed to fill her with joy. She and Dad didn't buy old homes and work every weekend fixing them up because it was fun.

I didn't know what to say to her or what to do. I'd not been happy a few nights earlier when I'd been allowed only two pairs of shoes for school—everyday ones and sneakers for gym class.

At that moment I began to see into the secret things they hadn't told me, and I saw the value of their sacrifice in order to provide for their family.

CHALLENGES
GREAT AND
SMALL

The Wash House,
the Kitchen,
and the Garden

During my visits to Miriam's home, I like to chip in and help, but the Amish way of handling chores is quite different from my way.

For one thing, the Amish avoid gasoline-powered motors, electricity, and owning cars. Lawns are cut with push reel mowers. Transportation is provided by horse and buggy. Light comes from kerosene lamps or natural-gas lighting, similar to items Englischers use when camping out. When I go to Miriam's, I take a flashlight to use after the sun goes down.

In winter, Amish homes are heated by burning wood or by gas that comes into the home from a propane tank in the backyard. The propane also provides energy to heat the hot-water tank and keep the refrigerator running. Cooling a home in summer is managed through open windows and shade trees. When that doesn't work and it's too hot to sleep, people who have basements move to them.

When my youngest son first went with me to Miriam's, he was around eight. One of the benefits for me was the inability of the world to sneak into the home. I didn't have to monitor sitcoms, movies, computer games, or Internet usage. To my delight he loved every minute of his visits. The only thing he missed was a fan blowing at night, not just to add a little coolness but also to block the noise of the farm. Who knew cows, horses, and donkeys were so talkative at night? I'd lived in a farming community in Maryland while growing up, and we had a few cows, horses, and chickens, but we kept our windows shut year-round, and in our two-hundred-year-old home, we ran several window-unit air conditioners all summer.

The aim for self-sufficiency is important to the Amish, as is their desire to live separate from the world. Natural gas– and solar-powered items make life a little easier, but they don't alter the Amish way of life— only their workload. The use of natural gas and solar power are in line with the goal of staying close to home and hearth. They don't pull people away from their community the way electricity or owning vehicles would.

I began my first morning at Miriam's home by making beds, straightening rooms, and gathering dirty clothes. I'm sure she doesn't allow her usual visitors to do those things, but I convinced her that I needed the experience in order to save her time in explaining how the Amish perform their tasks. She was all for that, and I could hardly blame her. I'm sure she could have washed and hung a week's worth of laundry in the time it had taken her to explain the processes over the phone or in a letter.

On that first day I took my load of dirty clothes to the wash house. This small room is attached to her home through an enclosed hallway; it also has an outdoor entrance/exit that opens toward the clothesline. Together Miriam and I sorted the laundry into piles—whites, black aprons and some pants, and dresses by pale or dark color. Because the wringer washer tends to break buttons, the men's shirts and pants went into a pile of their own, regardless of their color. Since the Amish don't use zippers, most pants have a fair number of buttons.

She turned on the hot water in a mud sink and ran an attached hose into the basin of the wringer washer. As the tub began to fill, she sent her daughter up to the *Daadi Haus* (grandfather's house—pronounced *daw'-dee*), where Miriam's in-laws live, to ask her father-in-law to get the air compressor running. She said it was difficult to start and he knew how. The machine runs off compressed air, which is powered by a generator. I couldn't possibly explain how that thing works. All I know is that her father-in-law did what he needed to, and soon a very loud washer began agitating.

Almost all Old Order Amish homes have a wringer washer, usually powered by diesel fuel. Clothes are run through an agitation cycle. The model Miriam and I used has a switch for turning on the wringer washer, and if we didn't turn it off, like the time we were interrupted by visitors, it would run all day or until the compressor ran out of air.

To keep the buttons on the men's shirts and pants from breaking, we rinsed them in clean water and wrung them out by hand. We ran the rest of the clothes through a wash cycle and then through the wringer. After that I filled the mud sink with clean, warm water and dipped the clothes up and down until they were as soap free as possible. After running each piece back through the wringer again, I tossed the articles into a basket to be hung on the clothesline. Memories of watching my mom haul laundry out to the clothesline year after year flooded my thoughts.

Laundry is hung to dry on a clothesline year-round, and depending on the day of the week, clotheslines are often full. In wet weather laundry is either postponed until a dry day or is hung on lines in the basement or on wooden racks inside the home.

During a break from laundry, I went into the kitchen to get a glass of cold water and caught a glimpse of Miriam's foot-pedal sewing machine. I found this amazing since Amish mothers and daughters make all the outer clothing for everyone in the family, from infants' gowns to brides' dresses to burial clothes. (Undergarments and socks are usually store bought.)

My heart turned a flip as I ran my hands across the well-worn oak cabinet. How many pieces of clothing had been sewn on that machine and for how many years? I didn't ask. It seemed too private. But I noticed a piece of burgundy fabric lying beside the sewing machine, waiting for her to have time to finish making the dress for her daughter.

At least once a week, Amish mothers will set up an ironing board and iron the cotton shirts. An old-fashioned pressing iron, usually made of cast iron, is heated by placing it facedown on a wood-burning stove or over a low flame on a gas stove. When it's hot, they iron. When it cools down, they heat it back up. Some Amish women use lighter-weight, modern irons, but they remove the electric cord and heat them in the same manner as an old-fashioned pressing iron.

The delicate organdy prayer caps the Amish women wear are washed by hand and require careful handling and pressing.

A lot of Amish kitchens have two stoves: one gas and one wood. Gas stoves are heated with kerosene (called oil) or propane.

Miriam's beautiful, shiny, pale green and white wood stove is nearly a hundred years old. She keeps a small box beside it filled with kindling, recycled cardboard boxes, and old newspapers. In winter she keeps the wood stove going all day and cooks meals on it. In spring and fall, she'll start a small fire in the morning to knock the chill out of the air and to percolate coffee, but by noon she lets it go out. She doesn't use it at all in summer.

Cooking on a wood stove presents special challenges. There's no way to turn the heat down, so Miriam moves items to spots where she knows the stove isn't as hot, or she holds the skillet an inch from the heat while the food finishes cooking. A wood stove's oven heats unevenly as well. So Miriam times the rotation of each item that's baking, whether it's casseroles or meats. She doesn't even try to bake bread or cookies in the wood stove. That's a job for the gas stove, which sits just a few feet away.

Miriam uses a stovetop waffle iron, popcorn popper, and percolator. I own a top-of-the-line coffee maker and an electric grinder to grind the coffee beans, but, in my opinion, Miriam's stovetop percolator makes the world's best coffee. At home I drink one cup of coffee in the morning and don't want any more. When I stay with Miriam, I drink about six cups—and always want more! Of course, that's partly because she cooks breakfast in shifts—a necessity to get everyone fed and out the door on schedule. By the time her youngest ones are off to school, she's cooked three or four rounds of breakfast, and I've enjoyed a cup of coffee and a chat with each group.

Every spring Amish women plant gardens that produce enough vegetables to sustain the family throughout the year. The gardens are tilled by hand or with horse-drawn equipment. If a garden yields too much of any one thing, the women may set up roadside stands and sell their extra produce. If there's a food they don't grow themselves, they'll buy bushels of it from a farmers' market and can it.

I hadn't realized that people even can meat until I became friends with Miriam. Her husband and five sons hunt according to the season and bring home meat that she cans for the winter.

Even with all their gardening, farming, and hunting, the Amish do purchase items like toiletries, cereal, sugar, and flour from local grocery stores. Although many homes have the means to make butter, not every family chooses to do so. Whatever they don't make, they buy.

Miriam has a sister-in-law, Maryann, who bakes dozens of loaves of zucchini bread each week throughout the winter for a famers' market. So Miriam gives her all her leftover zucchini, and every year Maryann cans between two and three hundred quarts of fresh zucchini.

Here's Maryann's zucchini bread recipe.

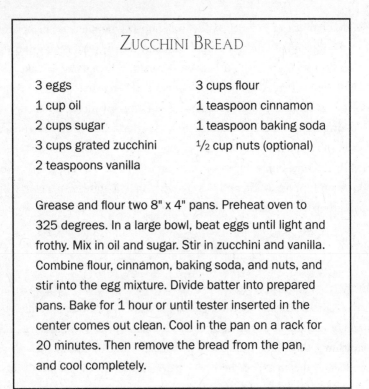

Zucchini Bread

3 eggs
1 cup oil
2 cups sugar
3 cups grated zucchini
2 teaspoons vanilla

3 cups flour
1 teaspoon cinnamon
1 teaspoon baking soda
1/2 cup nuts (optional)

Grease and flour two 8" x 4" pans. Preheat oven to 325 degrees. In a large bowl, beat eggs until light and frothy. Mix in oil and sugar. Stir in zucchini and vanilla. Combine flour, cinnamon, baking soda, and nuts, and stir into the egg mixture. Divide batter into prepared pans. Bake for 1 hour or until tester inserted in the center comes out clean. Cool in the pan on a rack for 20 minutes. Then remove the bread from the pan, and cool completely.

From Miriam

After my garden is fertilized, plowed, and tilled—which is around the last of March when all chance of frost is past—the fun begins.

Potatoes are the first items I plant. I take a twenty-pound bag of potatoes and cut each potato into fourths, making sure every piece has an eye in it. If the piece doesn't have an eye, a potato plant won't grow. Twenty pounds of "potato seed" will feed my family of six all winter long.

Onion sets are planted early too.

Between the middle and end of April, I plant green beans and sweet corn, two fifteen-foot rows of each. A few weeks later I'll plant a few more rows of corn. Staggering the planting allows us to have fresh sweet corn on the cob throughout the season as well as enough for freezing for winter use. I don't can sweet corn because it spoils too easily in jars.

At the beginning of May, I buy my tomato and pepper plants at the local greenhouse. My daughters-in-law start their tomato and pepper plants from tiny seeds. I haven't had the patience for that art yet. I'm not the aggressive gardener that some of our people are, but I do enjoy gardening. This year I have twelve tomato plants. That should be enough to can dozens of quarts of plain juice and dozens of quarts of both pizza and spaghetti sauce.

Planting and harvesting red beets and cucumbers are a must since we serve them at our church dinners. It takes about eight quarts of pickled beets and eight quarts of pickles for each church meal we host at our home, plus I can extra for our own use.

About that same time in May, or sometimes toward the middle of the month, I plant carrots and zucchini.

Throughout the growing season, the garden requires a lot of weeding, hoeing, cultivating, and more weeding. I like to do the weeding first thing in the morning while it's cool and I have the most energy.

When there's a dry spell, I take time each day to water the garden. Our water supply comes from a well on our property. It runs into the home through pipes and out using faucets and spigots. I pull the sprinkler into the garden and let it run for an hour or two each morning and each evening in dry weather, moving the sprinkler to different parts of the garden as needed. I enjoy working in the garden by myself, but if I get behind in weeding, the children help me. Even Daniel and the older boys pitch in on occasion.

The potato plants are dead by mid-August, but the potatoes themselves can stay in the ground and be harvested as needed until mid-September. Most of my garden items—corn, carrots, green beans—stop producing by the end of August, but I'll usually have fresh tomatoes and peppers until the frost hits in late October or early November.

Although I devote a lot of time to the garden, I know that even the best-cared-for gardens would produce nothing without God's blessings of sunshine and rain. That's another reminder of how helpless we are and how dependent on Him.

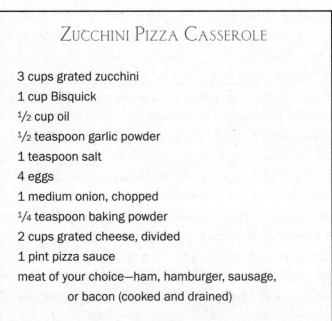

When there is an overabundance of a vegetable from my garden, that's a great time to pull out veggie-friendly recipes. This one is a family favorite.

Zucchini Pizza Casserole

3 cups grated zucchini
1 cup Bisquick
$1/2$ cup oil
$1/2$ teaspoon garlic powder
1 teaspoon salt
4 eggs
1 medium onion, chopped
$1/4$ teaspoon baking powder
2 cups grated cheese, divided
1 pint pizza sauce
meat of your choice—ham, hamburger, sausage,
       or bacon (cooked and drained)

Mix together all ingredients except 1 cup of the grated cheese, the pizza sauce, and the meat. Spread in a greased 9" x 13" pan, and bake at 350 degrees for 30–35 minutes. Remove from the oven, and top with pizza sauce, the remaining cup of grated cheese, and the meat. Bake at 350 degrees for another 15 minutes or until heated throughout.

THE FLIP SIDE

And the Lord make you to increase and
abound in love one toward another, and
toward all men, even as we do toward you.

—1 THESSALONIANS 3:12

From Cindy

I'd been married a little more than a year when Tommy did something that absolutely infuriated me. I stood in my kitchen dumping biscuit ingredients into a bowl while he sat in the living room reading the newspaper. It was all I could do to keep from throwing the bowl full of flour and buttermilk across the room—preferably at his head! Instead, I plunged my hands into the dough and mixed with indignation.

I managed to maintain outward restraint, but inwardly I rehashed how wrong he was. My list of grievances grew longer and longer until I thought I was going to explode.

How could he just sit in the next room, enjoying his newspaper, ignoring how wrong he was? He'd made some halfhearted apology without even trying to understand the scope of what he'd done wrong. I slung the dough over, tossed a little fresh flour on it, and pounded my fists into it again. *Can't he see how wrong he is?* I fumed.

A voice of reason said, *Everybody's wrong at one time or another. You were wrong just a few weeks ago.*

I wasn't this *wrong! And it'd make my life a whole lot easier if he was never wrong.*

If he were always right, you'd be the only one in this relationship who was ever wrong.

I stopped kneading the dough and mulled that over. If he were never wrong, he'd be like a god. And I'd be at fault way too often.

Anger drained from me. I dumped the overworked dough into the trash, rinsed the bowl, and started fresh—this time thinking how awful it would be to live a lifetime with a person who was always right, making me the only one who was ever wrong.

Thanks to that revelation, I've never become as angry as I was that day.

The funny thing is, within a year or two, I couldn't even remember what he'd done that had made me so furious. I only remember the lesson—that we are both imperfect, both in need of correction, grace, and forgiveness from each other.

Over the years I've had seasons of needing more grace and forgiveness than he did. At other times he's needed more than I have. But neither of us has had to grant more forgiveness than God grants to each of us every day.

Below is an Amish biscuit recipe that is similar to the one I was using that day. Tip: If you overknead the dough, you'll have a flat and tough biscuit. And if you overdo the anger, you'll have a flat and tough life.

BUTTERMILK BISCUITS

2 cups all-purpose flour
3 tablespoons sugar
$1/4$ teaspoon cream of tartar
$1/4$ teaspoon salt
4 teaspoons baking powder
$1/2$ cup butter or margarine, chilled and cut into pieces
$2/3$ cup buttermilk, chilled

Preheat oven to 450 degrees. Combine dry ingredients in a large bowl. Cut in butter or margarine until the mixture resembles coarse crumbs. Make a well in the center, and add the buttermilk. Combine until a sticky dough forms.

Place the dough on a floured surface, and gently fold it over itself three or four times to make layers. Pat the dough out to about $1/2"$ thickness. Dip a round cutter or the rim of a drinking glass in flour, and then cut the dough into rounds. Gently knead the scraps together, and repeat the process until all the dough is used. Bake on an ungreased cookie sheet for 10–12 minutes; biscuits will be light golden brown on top and bottom. Makes six to eight biscuits.

From Miriam

With mixed emotions my sister Rebecca put away the last of the groceries in her pantry. Someone had left another box of food on her doorstep. Wiping tears away, she bowed her head in gratitude.

When the economy crashed, her husband's work had slowed. So, like the rest of the country, the Esh family tightened their belts and tried to get by with less. They were staying afloat until their thirteen-year-old invalid daughter, Lydia, needed medical attention.

Lydia was born with Rett syndrome, and over the years she has developed scoliosis (curvature of the spine). Hospitalization and surgery were recommended to correct the problem, but first Lydia needed to be x-rayed. To the surprise of Rebecca and her husband, this required an hour and a half of sedation and a full MRI, which resulted in a shocking bill.

Family and friends, Amish and English alike, rallied around them. One generous family offered to host a benefit supper providing fun for the whole community, lots of great food, volleyball games for the youth, and great fellowship.

Normally Rebecca enjoyed attending these suppers. She was always the first one to support a good cause. But when the tables turned and she was on the receiving end, she discovered how hard it can be to accept other people's hard-earned money. Money she would most likely never be able to repay.

As Rebecca struggled with this, the thought came to her mind that this situation resembled the plan of salvation. God's grace is not something you earn, and you can never repay it. You simply accept it.

As she reflected further on this, she realized that God's love is often carried out through His people. God had just showered her and her family with more love than she could ever imagine. And, as with His grace, all she needed to do was accept it and be grateful.

LIFE INTERRUPTED

> That which was from the beginning, which
> we have heard, which we have seen with our
> eyes, which we have looked upon, and our
> hands have handled, of the Word of life.
>
> —I JOHN 1:1

From Miriam

When Joseph and Mary desperately needed a place for the night, innkeepers turned them away again and again. All the inns were full. Finally, acknowledging Mary's obvious needs, someone offered them the use of his stable.

We like to think that if Mary, in labor, knocked on our door, surely we'd give her our own bedroom. We certainly wouldn't turn her away completely. But how often do we miss great opportunities? I can think of a few I've missed—or almost missed. One especially stands out in my mind.

Several years ago after having had company all weekend, I was anxious to get back to filling the orders I'd received for my crafts. I have a craft business and make all sorts of items to sell at craft fairs or to put on consignment in various stores. I was already behind on several agreed-upon completion dates, but before I could sit down to resume my previous week's work, an English neighbor stopped in and asked if we'd give her visiting nephew a buggy ride.

I am ashamed to admit it now, but for a second I felt annoyed. What did she think we were, an amusement park? Not only was the timing bad, but our horse was out in the far end of the pasture.

I was about to say, "Sorry," when I noticed her leading the boy carefully by his hand, watching his every step. The child was blind. Shame washed over me for thinking I was too busy.

As quickly as I could, I fetched the horse and hitched it to the buggy, then gave that little boy the ride of his life. With each squeal of delight that escaped from his lips, I promised myself to never hold my work as a higher priority than a golden opportunity to serve the Lord in a simple act of hospitality.

From Cindy

In 2002, years before my first book was under contract, my youngest son and I boarded Amtrak in Georgia at midnight, and we made our first visit to Miriam's home. Four years later, as I started writing the second book in the series, *When the Morning Comes,* I expected my earlier traveling experience to be sufficient research for the opening scene, when Hannah stepped off that same train. But each time I tried writing the opening, it didn't sound the way I wanted it to. I'd write five chapters and delete five chapters, over and over again. It finally became clear that I needed to see and feel what Hannah would as she stepped off that train. I had to see the Alliance, Ohio, depot in person.

So I made plans to board Amtrak in Gainesville, Georgia, and change trains as needed until I arrived in Alliance. I checked online to see how long the ride was and discovered that the train would arrive in Alliance around two in the morning. I could deal with that.

But as I attempted to finalize my itinerary, I kept hitting dead ends. I called Amtrak several times and spoke with different people, trying to locate a cab company or bus line so I could get to a motel after arriving. No one was able to help me, and I couldn't chance landing in Ohio at two in the morning without a solid plan.

I told my husband we needed to drive there. Being the agreeable man I married thirty years ago, he took my word for it and made arrangements to take time off from work.

A few weeks later we pulled into the Alliance train depot. The night sky swirled with snow, but the thin white blanket couldn't hide the eeriness of the run-down, abandoned building. A white and blue sign near the tracks indicated a pay phone. I climbed out of the car. Snow and gravel crunched under my feet as I walked toward the sign. The wind whipped through my coat as if it wasn't there.

I reached the sign but didn't find a phone.

As I stood at that bleak, desolate depot, Hannah's life unfolded before my eyes, and I couldn't take notes fast enough. By the end of our week's stay in Alliance, I knew more than how a traumatized teenage Amish girl managed to survive away from her home, family, and community. I also knew who she became and why.

I found Hannah. And all it took was getting to the place where I could see what she'd seen, hear what she'd heard, and feel what she'd felt. Basically we'd driven to the place where I could slip into her shoes and walk a mile.

May I be that willing to make the necessary sacrifices to walk in a friend's, a neighbor's, or even a stranger's shoes. I must figuratively, and sometimes physically, remove myself from the comforts of home, travel to wherever that person is, and allow my heart to open to his or her reality. No judgment, no frustration, and no coldness of heart allowed. Just an open mind and heart and a willingness to be fully present as I offer an embrace as God has embraced me.

Love and Prayer
and So Much More

Ask, and it shall be given you; seek, and ye
shall find; knock, and it shall be opened
unto you: For every one that asketh receiveth;
and he that seeketh findeth; and to him that
knocketh it shall be opened.

—Matthew 7:7–8

From Cindy

At times, when my family is still asleep or no one is home, I walk the
floors of my home with my Bible open, and I pray Scripture. It does more
for my inner joy than if I went on extended exotic trips, were the perfect
size, or had a maid—none of which are a part of my life!

It gives me peace and stirs such hope that by the time I'm done, I
often feel as if I *can* move mountains, both through prayer and through
sheer determination. But that prayer time is never about seeking immediate healing for anyone, resolution to financial needs, or direct answers.

There's a time for those prayers, but when I walk the floors praying
Scripture, it's about praying for my family's hearts (and my own) to be
strengthened, for our eyes to be opened to more of who God is, and for
the meaning of true success to take root or grow stronger in us. It's like
speaking a blessing over us. I believe the influence of these Scripture
prayers will extend to God's moving in our lives in the months, years, and
decades ahead. I believe I'm speaking blessings that will continue to

unfold long after I'm gone from this planet. I'm praying and believing for the overall welfare, preservation, and long-term relationship with God of my children, their spouses (or future spouses), and their children, and their children's children. I have spent a lot of years praying for the safety—physically, emotionally, and spiritually—of my future daughters-in-law.

Because I'm not asking for little favors, and I'm not emotionally stressed about something happening in a person's life right then, and I'm not needing God to rescue someone—immediately!—it seems that I enter a zone of faith unlike any other prayer time.

I make the scriptures personal, but when I began doing this, there were no books about praying His Word. At first I found it hard to speak such things so boldly over my loved ones. How could I dare take His Word and speak the power of it over little peons like us? It felt as if I thought we were worth more than we actually are.

But I continued the prayer time, wrestling with feelings of inappropriateness toward God. One day while praying, I began to understand. When Christ died on that cross, He made it clear that nothing was too good for us. After all, He'd been brutalized and humiliated to give all little peons everything good God has to offer.

Psalm 127:1–2 says, "Except the LORD build the house, they labour in vain that build it: except the LORD keep the city, the watchman waketh but in vain. It is vain for you to rise up early, to sit up late, to eat the bread of sorrows." I consider the house in those verses to be the heart, soul (the mind and will and many emotions), and body of those I love, and I boldly proclaim to Him that I can do my absolute best for my children, and it's nothing, zilch, nada, unless He's the one doing the building and protecting each area. If I give my children too much, they could become spoiled or feel superior to others. If I give them too little, they could resent it or feel inferior. We all know there's no perfect balance in anything on this earth. That's where God moves in and balances everything out through His work in our hearts, souls, and bodies.

My prayer for each one of you comes from Ephesians: May the eyes of your understanding be enlightened that you may know the hope of His calling, and may you know the riches of the glory of His inheritance in you (see 1:18). May He grant, according to the riches of His glory, that you be strengthened with might by His Spirit in your inner person. Because Christ dwells in your heart by faith, may you be rooted and grounded in love and able to comprehend with all saints the love of Christ. Now to Him who is able to do exceeding abundantly above all that I ask or think, according to the power that works within us, unto Him be the glory throughout all the ages (see 3:16–21).

From Miriam

The walk down the lane that ran through the field to my sister's house was quiet and refreshing in the early morning sunshine. After closing the gate that divided our adjoining farms, I walked along the line of trees to her home.

As I entered Sarah's kitchen, the aromas of fresh-perked coffee and just-baked chocolate-chip cookies welcomed me. I found my sister sitting at the table with a mug of coffee in her hands. I felt somewhat guilty for disturbing her quiet time, but I knew that indulging in a warm chocolate-chip cookie would ease most of that guilt.

Opening her cupboard to get a cup for myself, I noticed her unusual mug collection. My sister has never been one to put much stock in matching sets of beautiful dishes. Instead, she appreciates unique pieces, especially coffee mugs. Many have been given to her by friends or relatives. Several she received as wedding favors. Giving mugs engraved or printed with the names of the bride and groom and their wedding date is common among the Amish.

During my sister's morning quiet time, she prays for the person or couple who gave her the mug she's using. No one but God knows how many prayers she's prayed over those mugs. Or how many of her prayers have been answered. But I believe one of those answers came fourteen months ago when I was blessed with a healthy grandson.

My son and daughter-in-law had been childless for the first three years of their marriage. For an Amish family, this is both rare and problematic. From our earliest memories, three things are ingrained in the Amish: God, community, and family. Careers and prestige are not valued. Children are. A job is important only because that's how a family is supported. Formal education isn't important; learning is, but the point of all knowledge is to understand God's Word as much as possible, to be a help to the community, and to take care of the family financially.

We're taught that beauty fades, physical strength drains as age progresses, and youthful desires disappear. To the Amish, the only thing on this earth that truly lasts is posterity—future generations. When a couple gets married, they and the entire community anticipate that the new couple will be expecting soon—perhaps within a few months and surely by the couple's first anniversary.

But my daughter-in-law's infertile state hadn't daunted my sister. For months she drank her morning coffee from the mug her nephew had given her at his wedding. And every day she prayed that God would open his wife's womb, fully believing that the miracle of life would happen in God's timing.

And indeed it did.

A Day in the Life

She looketh well to the ways of her household, and eateth not the bread of idleness.

—Proverbs 31:27

From Cindy

From ceiling to floor, my home almost glistened with cleanliness. My toddler was in his highchair, and I was feeding him homemade vegetable stew. Even though I was expecting a second child, I was dressed as if I were about to head out the door for church.

In the middle of this picture-perfect moment, my aunt Lillie Mae dropped in. She'd come by to pick up an infant bouncer that belonged to one of her daughters. Although we saw each other at other times, it was her only visit to my home. Afterward she told people I was an amazing homemaker, cook, and mom.

A few months later a neighbor came by unannounced. I had two little ones by that point. I'd been up half the night with the newborn, and I was running a low-grade fever from a recent bout with the flu. My home looked totally disheveled, and I looked even worse. This was my neighbor's first visit...and her last. The image she left with was completely opposite of my aunt's.

When I consider the stark contrast of those two events, I am reminded never to feel too good (or too bad) about the snapshot image someone has of me or my home. And I refuse to evaluate someone else by what I observe in a snippet of time—good or bad. More importantly, I realize that self-worth cannot be based on another person's opinion. It must come from our own hearts. And if we don't have a balanced viewpoint of who we are? If we often feel buried under condemnation and guilt? Then remember what 1 John 3:20 says: if our own hearts condemn us, we know that God is greater than our hearts.

From Miriam

My husband and I had an appointment at our home with a loan officer one afternoon. Wanting to make a good impression, my husband insisted that the milking facilities look their best. That was my job.

After a hurried breakfast that morning, leaving the dishes and my kitchen in a complete mess, I rushed out to the barn to shine the place. While the cows contentedly chewed their hay in their milking stalls, I swept and scrubbed the long hallway between the two rows of Holsteins and spread barn snow. Several hours of hard work later, I trudged up to the house, relieved that I'd finished the job before the man arrived.

When I opened the door of the house, the children greeted me, still in their pj's and swollen diapers. Hearing voices from inside, I peeped around the corner and saw my husband sitting at the table with two well-dressed men. The meeting was already in progress, and it was taking place in my dirty kitchen. I was too embarrassed to greet our guests properly, so I skulked through the kitchen like a stray cat.

The gentlemen never did go to the barn or the milk house, which had far more shine than my home. My only consolation was that if I ever met those classy people again, they wouldn't recognize me.

Though the house was a mess, I hadn't been idle. On the contrary, I'd worked my fingers to the bone…just not on what those men saw.

God knew my intentions and my heart, and I found comfort in knowing that not only had I done exactly what my husband had asked of me but I had done my very best. But even with those truths in my heart, the situation was embarrassing.

Looks can indeed be deceiving. People may look a certain way on the outside when in their hearts they're completely different. This incident reminded me not to judge a book by its cover or a woman by her kitchen.

I Am Who I Am

Now ye are the body of Christ, and members
in particular.... Are all apostles? are all
prophets? are all teachers? are all workers of
miracles?

—1 Corinthians 12:27, 29

From Miriam

The busyness of today can shape our tomorrows. For better or worse, who
and what I yield to today will affect who I become. We can't accept every
opportunity that comes our way, and we can't always know which opportunity is the best to pursue or which doors we should walk through and
which ones we shouldn't.

Over the years I've discovered that I'm quite gullible, especially when
it comes to bargains or a great sales pitch. Yet at the same time, I trust very
few people, particularly when my children or grandchildren are involved.

Knowing I can trust God in any circumstance is a great help. He will
guide me in the right direction, through the right doors, if I only will
ask…and then listen for His answer.

From Cindy

When I was young, I couldn't keep up with anything. If I touched it, I
lost it. The worst thing was taking the time to do homework and then
misplacing it before turning it in. Ugh! So when my teenagers inherited
that wonderful trait, I couldn't complain.

I got numerous calls from the boys when they were in high school, describing what they'd left at home and where they wanted me to take it so they could get it. Even if I couldn't remember the last time I'd forgotten something at home, I always told them, "I won't get angry with you as long as you don't get angry with me when my turn comes."

One year I planned a birthday party at a bowling alley for my youngest son. The day of the party was one of those superbusy days, and I was relieved when I finally pulled into the bowling alley parking lot—on time and with my son, his bowling ball, and birthday cake.

My husband worked near the area, so he planned to meet us there. Justin was in college, and Adam was in high school—they planned to meet us there as well.

Once inside, I realized I'd forgotten the paper plates, napkins, cups, etc. The bowling alley had made their position clear: they'd provide pizza and drinks for the party, but everything else was my responsibility.

As Tyler's friends and their parents trickled in and started bowling, I called Justin with my request for paper plates and napkins. He told me he would pick them up on his way.

When I realized I'd forgotten candles for the cake, I called Adam. He agreed to pick them up.

Then I realized I'd forgotten the knife for cutting the cake. I called my husband. He was just about to leave work, and there was a knife in the office kitchen that he could bring.

Next I realized I'd forgotten the plastic eating utensils. And the ice cream. And a scoop. And matches for the candles. And…

I called Tommy and my older boys repeatedly, asking them to run to the store or our house for needed items.

Just as the pizza was brought to the tables, my husband and two older sons walked inside with big grins, obviously having met in the parking lot. They plunked their goods onto the table.

Tommy smiled. "I couldn't wait to get here and make sure you hadn't forgotten Tyler."

It was amusing, no doubt. But the truth is, every one of us has traits that are not fun and are rather embarrassing. When I'm tired of my faults, I comfort myself with the knowledge that I'm not the only one in this family with idiosyncrasies. We've found that the trick to keeping frustration and resentment from building is to choose to respect one another. We often accomplish this by naming what the person is good at while in the midst of dealing with their fault. And it also helps to not compare our strongest areas with their weakest areas.

CAN YOU HEAR ME NOW?

Hold fast the form of sound words, which
thou hast heard of me, in faith and love
which is in Christ Jesus.

—2 TIMOTHY 1:13

From Miriam

Our long winter evenings are usually spent in the living room with most
of us reading. Mark, age twelve, loves when I read to him.

One evening I read a book about how the West was settled after the
California gold rush in 1849.[2] I was amazed at all the effort and hard
work it took to do ordinary tasks and the progress that has been made in
the years since then. For instance, mail traveled by boat down the East
Coast and across the tip of South America to get to the West Coast. It
took a month to make the voyage.

In 1857 stagecoaches began transporting mail from St. Louis to San
Francisco, some 2,795 miles by the routes of that day. It took the stagecoach up to twenty days to deliver a letter and required lots of horse
power as well as man power.

In 1860 the pony express began offering the fastest mail delivery ever
attempted. They could deliver in half the time of a stagecoach.

After telegraph lines were strung from one end of the country to
the other in 1861, messages crossed the country in only minutes. What
progress!

Now here we are in the twenty-first century. I don't know much about computers, but I understand that with just a few taps of the fingers, an e-mail can travel anywhere in the world almost instantly. That's amazing! Our means of communication have surely come a long way. Although the Amish discourage the use of cell phones, fax machines, e-mail, and computers, even our means of communication have stepped up a notch or two over the years. We send a lot of letters and cards through the postal service, but the use of phones in a phone shanty and voice-mail messages left on a machine occur more and more. My sister Sarah and her husband were the last ones in our Amish community to build a phone shanty and get a phone. Since then we've written across-the-field notes less often.

Even with all this progress, one type of communication is and always has been better than all the others. I call it "knee mail." We can just *think* a prayer, and God receives it. No cell phone or computer is needed. No calls are ever dropped. You'll never get one back marked "not deliverable." God hears every single one of our prayers.

From Cindy

When my seventeen-year-old son asked permission to attend a concert at Atlanta's Music Midtown Festival, his eyes radiated excitement. More than 120 bands would perform on six stages, all within walking distance. Two of his friends were going, and they had an extra ticket for him. The oldest one would drive to the MARTA (rail/train) station, and they'd ride from there to midtown Atlanta.

I wasn't the least bit worried about Adam participating in any of the usual nonsense that occurs during these festivals, like drinking or drugs. However, I was a little apprehensive about the crowd. Nearly two hundred thousand people were likely to be there. Still, I couldn't refuse to let my son do everything that concerned me.

Tommy and I talked with all three boys, made sure the driver had a cell phone, gave clear instructions about staying together at all times, and granted our permission.

When Adam and his friends arrived at the concert, they found it even busier and more confusing than they'd expected. People pushed and shoved, determined to get close to the stages. The boys tried to stick together, but throngs of people kept pushing them farther apart until Adam lost sight of his friends.

Rain poured, making it hard to see and even harder to be heard as he called his friends' names. A mass of humanity pressed in on every side, and he had no clue how to get back to the MARTA station.

He asked several strangers if he could borrow a phone. He knew if he could reach his dad, Tommy would know how to get him out of that mess. But no one would hand him a cell phone when they could easily get separated.

Around eleven o'clock I received a call from my son's friends, telling me they'd lost track of Adam. My teenage boy was wandering around Atlanta, among throngs of people, in a downpour.

Tommy called our pastor at home and told him the situation. He prayed with us, then called others to pray. As the clock ticked on, my heart cried out to God for my son's safety.

While Adam was praying for a phone, he kicked something. Light seemed to come from the object, though it was hard to tell in the dark with wall-to-wall people surrounding him and pouring rain. He reached down to grab whatever it was, but someone unknowingly kicked it farther away. He went to his knees, felt around in the mud, and finally found it. He pulled it out. It was a cell phone!

We got his call around midnight. Screaming to be heard above the rain and the crowd, Tommy told him what landmarks to follow. Within twenty minutes Adam was on the right path toward the MARTA station. Tommy told him what station to get off at and promised he'd meet him there.

When they lost their connection, my husband made a beeline for the closest MARTA station, hoping that Adam had understood his directions. When he arrived, he found Adam there, waiting.

The next morning we called the numbers listed in that cell phone until we found someone who knew to whom the phone belonged. Moments later we heard from the owner, who was thrilled we'd found his phone. His employer had given it to him the day before, and he was worried what would happen when he told his boss he'd lost it.

We returned the young man's phone, immeasurably grateful for God's provision.

Miriam and I were talking about this incident one day, and she shared about Daniel and her being in the milking barn one summer afternoon. They had two young sons in the barn with them and a baby in the stroller. The children played quietly in a safe zone while Miriam and Daniel prepared the stalls and filled the troughs with feed. Before each milking time, some of the cows pressed against the gate, bumping the latch with their noses and licking it. They were hungry and full of milk and wanted inside!

After bedding a stall, Miriam looked up to see that a cow had loosened the latch, and all thirty cows were running inside. Her three-year-old son, Mervin, had wandered into the direct line of the oncoming cows, and she was too far away to reach him before the cows did. She didn't even have time to think a whole prayer, but she managed a cry to God for help.

In a flash their collie bounded into the barn, got between Mervin and the cows, and started barking furiously. The cows stopped cold. They couldn't back up because there were other cows behind them pushing them forward, but that gave Miriam the bit of time she needed to grab her little one and get out of the way.

Appropriately, the dog's name was Lassie.

When Adam was caught in a difficult situation, God provided a cell phone, but when Mervin was in danger, God didn't need modern technology in order to intervene.

Everything from scraping a knee to a full-blown tragedy will happen on this fallen planet, but I believe that God is constantly at work on our behalf. The New International Version says in John 10:10, "The thief comes only to steal and kill and destroy; I have come that they may have life, and have it to the full." In other words, in all circumstances He is on our side.

When Lack Hits Home

But my God shall supply all your
need according to his riches in glory
by Christ Jesus.

—Philippians 4:19

From Cindy

I stood in the backyard of our one-bedroom home, a toddler on my hip and a baby in my belly. The branches of our pecan trees were bare, and the threat of winter hung in the air.

Our house, like the hundreds around it, had been built before the Depression, and if the walls could've talked, they would have told of the many families who'd gone through boom times and hard economic times. My husband and I had lived there less than five years, and we'd experienced both sides of American life—making ends meet and not.

A few years earlier we'd both had good jobs, and we'd managed to put aside a little money. Before we were blessed with the birth of our first child, I left my job at the bank. We'd expected to be able to buy a three-bedroom home before he was born, but two weeks after I gave up my job, my husband was laid off from the steel plant. Three years and endless short-term jobs later, it was evident that this layoff was not temporary. The steel mills in America were struggling, and the United States was in a recession. The union was at an impasse with management. Benefits ran out. Our health insurance was canceled. Steady jobs, even at minimum wage, seemed impossible to find.

We'd slowly succumbed to the economy's circumstances and were living below the poverty level. The reality of our situation was never sharper than when I stood in the backyard that crisp November day. Bullying questions kept circling inside my head: *What about next week's food, the electric bill, the mortgage payment? And what about Christmas? Will the first Christmas our son is old enough to remember and understand be completely barren of gifts?*

We'd never had a credit card or a home-equity credit line, and even if we had been willing to take on the responsibility of getting one to help us make ends meet, we no longer qualified.

I'd become a Christian while expecting our first child, and in the midst of this present misery, praying without ceasing came as easily and naturally as breathing. Trusting what God would do and when wasn't nearly as effortless.

As the weeks crept toward Christmas, I continued to hone my skills of making a dollar stretch. My husband worked whatever odd jobs he could find.

Christmas Eve came, and we had a roof over our heads, wood in the wood stove, and a well-used artificial tree set up. We clung to hope, believing that times would surely get better. Tommy and I voiced to each other what we had to be thankful for. But after we tucked our son into bed on Christmas Eve, we sat in silence. Not in pools of despair, but in an ocean of hurt.

I went to the cabinet above the refrigerator, pulled out a gift, and placed our son's only present under the tree—a ten-inch plastic horse I'd bought at a yard sale for twenty-five cents. I was relieved that our son was too young to understand that there should be more for him when he woke on Christmas morn.

As we sat in our living room watching the wealthy celebrate Christmas on television, we heard bells jingle. Someone outside yelled, "Ho, ho, ho. Merry Christmas." I figured one of the neighbors must be playing Santa Claus, but then there was a loud knock on our front door.

When I opened the door, freezing air whipped into our home. I stepped onto the front porch and looked around, but no one was there. Then I saw several out-of-place things: a handmade wooden rocking horse; a small box of brightly colored, gently used toys; and a brown bag containing groceries, including a canned ham, vegetables, and store-bought rolls.

My heart soared, and my mind crowded with so many thoughts I couldn't settle on just one. Had someone left these items on the wrong doorstep? Then I noticed that our names were written on the grocery bag.

In that moment strength poured into me, and I understood that poverty could not conquer love, smother hope, or hold us hostage forever. God was behind the scenes, working through the hearts and lives of those who carried love.

That wasn't our last penniless year. We had another really tough winter the following year. But then my husband received a job opportunity in another state. In the spring we moved to Georgia—our land of new beginnings.

When my husband received his first paycheck from his new job, our grocery money instantly tripled. We hadn't stepped into utopia. We still had to sell the house in Alabama and make up for every partially paid utility bill. My husband worked fourteen-hour days, but we were still so far behind that I feared we might not be able to give our children all they'd need in life.

Still, I knew we didn't get out of the last mess on our own. And we weren't facing the future on our own either. Contentment demanded that we trust in the God who had provided and would continue to take care of us.

From Miriam

Standing inside the Christian Aid Ministries building with about ten women from my church, I put another pile of clean clothes on the long wooden table. Some of the women had spent days washing and drying the clothes.

The ceiling fan overhead made rhythmic humming sounds as it circulated the air around us and we sorted used clothes. Others sewed on missing buttons and repaired an occasional hem or seam. We separated men's from women's clothes, boys' from girls', and toddlers' from infants'. I especially enjoyed matching outfits for the children.

At the end of the room, dozens of additional bags of freshly washed and dried clothing awaited our attention. These clothes were then placed in nylon bags to be shipped to poor countries such as Romania, Ukraine, Nicaragua, and Africa—all under the auspices of Christian Aid Ministries.

As I worked, my mind wandered to what dear child might receive this outfit or that one, and even though I knew it was against the rules, I longed to slip a treat or surprise into the pockets in the hopes of cheering up some little boy or girl far away. It reminded me of a story I once read about a young mother doing missionary work in a very poor foreign country. Food and necessities were scarce among the natives as well as in her own home.

One day a native woman knocked on the young mother's door and asked for a bar of soap. Cleanliness was their only tool to fight diseases. The missionary feared for her family as her supply was low. She had just one bar left besides the thin sliver she was currently using, which would last only a few more days. And the next shipment wasn't due for months.

Desperately wanting to help, the missionary knew what she needed to do. Breathing a prayer heavenward, she gave away her last precious bar of soap. Seeing the look of pure joy on the lady's face, she knew she had done the right thing.

A few days later a shipment was delivered to their village, but soap was not among the supplies. However, on the next laundry day, when this missionary woman opened a new box of laundry detergent, she found a free bar of soap inside. Every box after that contained another precious bar of soap. Nothing less than a modern-day miracle.

It's like Elijah's story in the Bible.

When Elijah asked a widow for a piece of bread, she told him she had nothing baked and had only a handful of flour and a bit of oil left. She said to him, "I am gathering sticks to build a fire to bake the last of it, for myself and my son."

Elijah said, "Don't be afraid. Go and do as you have said. Only make me a loaf from it and bring it to me."

She agreed to do so, even though she knew it was her last. Afterward, whenever the widow baked again, the barrel of flour and the cruse of oil miraculously refilled. She and her household ate for many days. (See 1 Kings 17:10–16.)

The same God was looking out for both of these women, hundreds of years apart, and the same God is still watching over us and blessing us today.

Our God of compassion and mercy loves a generous giver whose heart is in the right place. He promises to reward such people, saying they shall lack nothing (see Proverbs 28:27).

LAUGHTER IN ODD PLACES

GAMES, PUZZLES, AND PLAYTIME

The Amish are known for being industrious, but they aren't workaholics. The children are taught to work, but they are also taught to enjoy free time. Without television or electronic games to distract them, the Amish have a healthy respect for leisure time.

Outdoor activities for children and youth include ice-skating, riding scooters, fishing, and playing hide-and-seek, baseball, volleyball, and horseshoes. The adults are free to join those activities whenever it suits them. There are no barriers against moms and dads playing.

I've seen older children on horses, racing through the fields. Nothing like a little competitive racing to cause moms' hearts to pound a little harder while the riders' laughter echoes off the hills. The Amish don't encourage competing, but a spirited effort is always good for laughs and good-natured teasing.

Games are popular—checkers, the Game of Life, Candy Land, Booby Trap, Jenga, and dominoes. Although many card games are off limits since their roots are tied to gambling, the Amish enjoy playing Old Maid, Dutch Blitz, Uno, Phase 10, and Go Fish.

They regularly have youth suppers where the adults provide a meeting place and a meal and the youth get together. In the summer, before the meal they might play volleyball, baseball, or horseshoes. In the winter, they stay indoors and play games or cards. If there's a Ping-Pong table in the house, the youth will put that to good use. After the meal they'll have a singing.

Some Amish enjoy putting puzzles together. The whole family usually gathers around to help. If neighbors stop in, Englischer or Amish, they are often invited to join in. When the puzzle is done, it may be mounted, framed, and given away or sold.

In the past the Amish didn't go on vacations and rarely traveled far from home. Today they will typically leave home to help others in times of need, even if they have to hire a driver or take a train or both, and some are beginning to enjoy the American pastime of vacations and sightseeing. Niagara Falls is a particularly popular destination. While traveling, they visit friends of friends along the way.

The Amish have an insatiable desire to enjoy life and each other, whether through work, games, or visiting. Here's a recipe that's sure to please any crowd.

FUDGE-FILLED BARS

3 cups oats
1 1/2 cups whole-wheat flour
1 cup nuts
1 cup brown sugar
1 teaspoon baking soda
3/4 teaspoon salt
1 cup butter, melted

Filling:
2 tablespoons butter
1 1/2 cups M&M'S, divided
1 can condensed milk

Mix together oats, flour, nuts, brown sugar, baking soda, salt, and melted butter. Reserve 1 1/2 cups of crumbs. Press remaining crumbs into a jelly-roll pan. Bake 10 minutes at 350 degrees.

For the filling, melt the 2 tablespoons of butter over low heat, stir in 1 cup of M&M'S, and cook until melted. (Some coating will remain.) Remove from the heat, and stir in the condensed milk. Then spread over the baked layer, staying a 1/2" away from the edges. Top with reserved crumbs and 1/2 cup of M&M'S; press together lightly. Bake until golden brown, about 20 minutes. Cool for approximately thirty minutes, and then cut into bars.

In a Cellar
or up a Tree

It is better to trust in the LORD than to put
confidence in man.

—PSALM 118:8

From Miriam

Like passing plates of steaming meat and vegetables at the dinner table,
we often pass stories around during mealtime. Since our oldest boys are
married with homes of their own, we rarely have the whole family here
for a meal, but when we do, it seems that the conversation is the main
course.

Recently I heard a story I hadn't thought of in a while, and it reminded me that when children get bored, adults usually pay the price.

My husband's sister Martha and his cousin Ruth Ann were at their
uncle Mannie's for a week while their dads were in Virginia. The girls
were around five years old and had run out of things to do. Ruth Ann
said, "I know! Let's peel potatoes!" Martha said, "I don't know how," but
Ruth Ann agreed to show her. So they began peeling potatoes—a big bag
of 'em—down in the cellar at an old sink Uncle Mannie had. Peelings
piled thick and fast. The potatoes were quite small once they had the
peelings off! They peeled a ten-gallon bucket (approximately fifty pounds
of potatoes) and put the dear little things in clear plastic bags. When they
showed the first bag full to Aunt Katie, she mumbled, "Uh-huh," and
went right on enjoying her after-dinner nap.

Guess what they had for every meal the rest of the week? Potatoes, of course, that Aunt Katie didn't have to peel!

Bored children often get into mischief, but sometimes they simply want to learn how to do what the adults do. If we want to instill a love of work, we can't wait until they're truly capable of being helpful. That will likely be too late. Catch them while they're still young and work looks exciting to them. Otherwise they'll grow up to be couch potatoes.

Aunt Katie would have benefited from this recipe that day.

CRUMB-TOP POTATOES

1/3 cup butter

3 or 4 large potatoes, cut in thin slices

1 1/2 cups sharp cheese, grated

3/4 cup crushed cornflakes

2 teaspoons salt

1 1/2 teaspoons paprika (optional)

Melt the butter in a jelly-roll pan in a 375-degree oven. Add the potatoes and turn once in the butter. Mix the remaining ingredients, and sprinkle over the top. Bake 30 minutes or until the potatoes are soft. Delicious!

From Cindy

I was in the backyard on a beautiful late fall day, playing with my two young sons. The Georgia air was a little nippy but nothing a sweater didn't fix.

When we heard a cat meowing, we began looking for it on our acre of land in the middle of seventy-plus acres of pastures and woods. We finally discovered our own cat, Charlie, up in a pine scrub tree that had no limbs close to the ground. Climbing it would be like trying to scale a slick pole, only with bark and ants.

Charlie looked and sounded pitiful, and the kids were sure he wanted down. So I did what every good mother does: assured them the cat would be fine until their father got home.

When Tommy arrived, looking as bedraggled and weary as the cat sounded, the boys led him to the tree while prattling frantically that he had to save Charlie. He studied the cat for a moment before assuring our boys that if the cat could climb up, he could climb down. So we went inside for supper.

As the sun went down, a chill settled over the house, so we started our first fire of the season in our wood stove. Tommy checked on the cat one more time and even tried to bribe it with people food, but Charlie stayed put.

When I woke the next morning, I went to the back door to call the cat. What I discovered was winter. A storm had come through, and the tree limbs drooped under a heavy load of ice. Charlie wasn't waiting at the back door as I thought he would be. I walked outside and heard a hoarse-sounding meow from atop the scrub pine. I hurried back to the bedroom to tell my husband.

In a flurry of activity, all four of us got dressed and rushed to the foot of the tree where Charlie was still perched, letting out his pitiful meow. My husband got a ladder out of the shed and leaned it against the frozen trunk.

After Tommy climbed the ladder as high as he could, he'd reached the lowest limb of the pine. He extended himself toward where the cat crouched. I knew we had to get Charlie down, but if Tommy fell... I didn't want to think about that.

Finally he got close enough to pick up Charlie. He yelled down at me, "Okay, I can get the cat. But how do I climb down this slippery tree with a frightened cat in one hand?"

I had an idea. I ran into the house and grabbed a sheet from the closet. Hurrying back, I yelled, "We'll stretch out the sheet, and you can drop the cat. We'll catch it."

He didn't look convinced, but we saw no other way to get the cat down safely.

Each boy held a corner of the sheet, and I grabbed the other two corners. We stretched out the sheet and stood there like firemen waiting to catch someone jumping from a burning building. I looked at the boys. "You have to hold on tight when Dad drops Charlie. Are you ready?" They gave me a half-frightened smile as they pulled on the sheet.

Tommy dropped the cat. The terrified, half-frozen fur ball hurtled toward us with his claws extended. But before Charlie reached the sheet, the two boys dropped their corners and took off running. A second later the cat landed.

All my life I'd heard that if you drop a cat, he'll always land on his feet. I guess if you drop a half-frozen cat from thirty feet up a scrub pine tree during an ice storm, the landing-on-his-feet rule doesn't necessarily apply.

Charlie hit the ground and took off running. Tommy climbed down safely. Soon both cat and owners were inside a toasty warm house, eating. Charlie slept soundly throughout the day, and his playfulness had returned by the next evening, and he never again climbed so far he couldn't get back down.

We've all ventured too far and gotten stuck at some time in our lives. And the ones who were supposed to help didn't, for whatever reason. Sometimes we have to endure that icy storm for a night, but we can be sure that God stands waiting in the storm for us, and when we finally let go and drop, He always holds tightly to the safety net.

Amish Friendship Bread

A friend loveth at all times, and a brother is
born for adversity.

—Proverbs 17:17

From Cindy

I was in the third grade when I made my first real friend in school. Until
that time I'd never asked anyone to come home to play with me unless
that person could walk to my house. But by the time I entered third
grade, we'd moved to a more rural area. When I asked my mom and dad
if my new friend could come over, they thought it sounded like a good
idea.

Our parents passed notes back and forth and worked out the details.
My friend and I were so excited! She couldn't spend the night, but she
could ride the bus to my house, and her dad would pick her up around
six o'clock.

We bounded off the bus that afternoon and waltzed inside, all giggles
and excitement. My mom greeted us, looking surprised when she met the
girl. We played in the backyard, walked to a nearby creek, and laughed
over the silliest things.

When my dad came home, he looked from my friend to my mom,
motionless for a moment before he smiled broadly and welcomed the girl.
When her dad arrived, his eyes grew large as his daughter introduced us.

A few minutes later I overheard the two dads talking. Only then did I finally understand my mother's surprise, my dad's amusement, and her dad's speechlessness.

It was the sixties, and my new friend was African American. I hadn't told my parents she was black, and she hadn't told her parents I was white. We were aware of the other one's skin color, but we didn't think it mattered. My parents had asked me if she was nice. They'd asked if she did her homework. They'd asked if she liked what my mom was going to fix for dinner the night she came. But no one asked what color skin she had.

I still remember the laughter as our fathers shook hands that day.

Every night in that era, the television news told of conflicts between blacks and whites. It might not have been comfortable for our dads to meet like that, but whatever either of them thought or felt, they were friendly during the exchange.

We moved a few months later. That's when I met my next best friend, a Plain Mennonite girl. After her my closest friend was first-generation Japanese. After her I had a native Hawaiian friend who practically lived with us on the weekends.

Perhaps it was coincidence that I had so many friends of different nationalities. Or maybe we had something in common. Because my family moved so often, I always felt out of place. Maybe that's why we gravitated toward one another. What I know for certain is that a good friend removes loneliness, and even when we go through a season where there are no earthly friends, God is always our friend (see John 15:15).

From Miriam

Sometime ago a friend stopped by my house with a plastic bag of the sourdough mixture called Amish Friendship Bread starter, along with the recipe and instructions. Years ago when everyone made bread, sourdough starter was a household staple. It is a continuous source or base, which can easily be shared or passed on. I'm not sure how it got the name Amish Friendship Bread. After all, it was an English friend who passed it to me.

After following the ten-day steps, I added more ingredients, mixed it well, then divided it into four separate bags, still having a separate amount of starter to feed and set aside. So I had one cup of starter to bake with and three to pass on to my friends. I looked forward to enjoying a new variety, chocolate-chip pudding.

Next I set out to find homes for the other three bags of starters. One friend didn't have time, one said it always flopped for her, and another said her family didn't care for it. So I tended to the starters each day while still trying to pass them along. After ten days, bake day came around again, and my starters now multiplied to sixteen, which would multiply to sixty-four in ten more days if I didn't find someone to adopt them.

Slightly frustrated I went to my mother to borrow bread pans and started baking. I baked for hours. I baked every last dollop of the sourdough mix and ended up with twenty loaves of delicious bread. And not a single starter.

While I worked through my recent frustration, I remembered that the best way to have a friend is to be one and the best way to strengthen a friendship is to do a kindness when it's not expected. So I started handing out baked friendship bread instead of bags of gooey starter. I gave all but two loaves, which I shared with my children. My friends, family, and I enjoyed the delicious bread as well as a fresh renewal in our kinship.

Amish Friendship Bread Starter

2 cups flour
2 cups warm water
1/4 cup sugar
1 packet yeast

Mix all ingredients with a wooden or plastic spoon in a nonmetallic bowl. Pour into a zippered plastic bag and continue with the following steps.

Amish Friendship Bread Instructions

Day 1:   Leave alone.
Day 2:   Squeeze bag several times.
Day 3:   Squeeze bag several times.
Day 4:   Squeeze bag several times.
Day 5:   Squeeze bag several times.
Day 6:   Add 1 cup flour, 1 cup sugar, 1 cup milk; squeeze bag until mixed.
Day 7:   Squeeze bag several times.
Day 8:   Squeeze bag several times.
Day 9:   Squeeze bag several times.
Day 10:   Pour the batter into a nonmetallic bowl. Add 1 cup each of flour, sugar, and milk. Mix with a wooden or plastic spoon. Pour four 1-cup starters into gallon-sized, zippered plastic bags. Give to friends along with the instructions, keeping one starter for yourself.

Then mix the following ingredients, and add to your portion of the starter:

1 cup oil

1 cup sugar

1 teaspoon vanilla

3 eggs

1^1/$_2$ teaspoons baking powder

1 teaspoon cinnamon

^{1}/$_2$ teaspoon salt

^{1}/$_2$ cup milk

^{1}/$_2$ teaspoon baking soda

2 cups flour

2 small boxes instant vanilla pudding mix

In a separate bowl, mix 1 teaspoon cinnamon with 4 tablespoons of sugar. Sprinkle into two 8" x 4" x 2^1/$_2$" greased bread pans. Pour batter into the pans. Bake at 350 degrees for 1 hour.

Chocolate pudding mix may be used instead of vanilla. You may also add chocolate chips, nuts, or raisins.

LAUNDRY, ANYONE?

He that is slow to anger is better than the
mighty; and he that ruleth his spirit than he
that taketh a city.

—PROVERBS 16:32

From Cindy

Tommy and I had two teens and a toddler when my family had to take
over all my duties. I'd had major surgery and was placed on full bed rest
for nearly four weeks.

My oldest kept up with his high school honors classes admirably. My
second son handled his homeschool lessons while watching his little
brother. My husband cooked all the meals, washed the dishes, and
cleaned the house without taking any time off from work. I felt proud of
my family for rising to the challenge. But I also had feelings that were
foreign to me. I felt left out and useless. Everyone was managing just fine
without me, and maybe my emotions were raw due to the circumstances,
but I hurt because no one really seemed to need me.

Finally the doctor gave his approval for me to be on my feet again.
The first day everything looked in great shape, so I went into the laundry
room to start a load of clothes. Surely there was dirty laundry.

Imagine my surprise when I opened the door to the tiny room and
found dirty clothes stacked everywhere! I stood in shock, staring at what
might be four weeks' worth of laundry. What was everyone wearing, the
cleanest of the dirty clothes?

I called my husband at work. He read the caller ID and answered with his usual "Hey, cutie. What's up?"

"I am."

"Good. Don't do too much. I think the place is in good shape."

"Uh, honey...what about the laundry?"

After a moment of silence, he gasped. "I never thought about that."

"You guys had to run out of things like underwear."

"Well, yeah. But I bought several packages for everyone. And socks too."

I thought, *You did that but forgot about the laundry?*

I'm not sure I was well enough to laugh as hard as I did, but it felt good to be on my feet again and to be assured that I was needed. It also gave me deeper empathy for people who deal with chronic illnesses or the adverse effects of aging and those who can't do for their family as they long to do.

And the month's worth of laundry certainly gave me fodder for harassing my good-natured husband.

From Miriam

One warm Sunday afternoon, on the spur of the moment, my family decided to go for a drive in our horse and buggy and visit my sister and her family. Our four youngest children, ages six to fifteen, scurried around, getting dressed in their best clothes. It was a challenge to find everyone's outfits in such short order, but soon we were in our buggy waiting on the last one, our fifteen-year-old son.

Minutes ticked by. Frogs croaked from the pond across the road. I drew a deep breath, enjoying the beauty of the late spring landscape in spite of the holdup.

Finally our son came to the upstairs window. "Mom, where are my dress pants?"

As an Amish mom, it's my responsibility to provide handmade clothes for the family. With five sons it's quite a job keeping everyone's clothes clean and mended. So this question wasn't unusual. However, in this instance I honestly couldn't remember what I'd done with my son's dress pants. I couldn't even recall whether he'd grown out of his latest pair.

I groaned. Surely he could find a pair that fit, at least well enough for today. I told him to check his brother's closet.

Seconds later he came to the window again. "Not there, Mom."

"Okay, check the mending pile. Maybe they had a button missing."

A few more minutes passed. I was starting to feel awful. Clearly I had not done my duty. I could think of several reasons I hadn't made new pants yet. We were in the middle of planting season, and some of my responsibilities—like keeping up with clothes—had been put on the back burner.

Just when I felt sure my husband's patience had reached its limit, the front door opened. Our son casually walked down the sidewalk toward the waiting buggy.

My jaw dropped. He was wearing a shirt and vest, dress shoes, black socks, and suspenders…but no pants. Yet he was strutting along as if everything were normal.

Hiding my amusement, I demanded, "Now, Mervin, you go right back in there and put on your hat!"

That stopped him in his tracks. The tension broke, and we all burst into laughter.

I was grateful that we could make light of something that could have ruined the start of our outing and caused bad feelings throughout the day.

THE COMFORT ZONE

Put on therefore, as the elect of God, holy and
beloved, bowels of mercies, kindness, humble-
ness of mind, meekness, longsuffering.

—COLOSSIANS 3:12

From Miriam

In the spring of 1975, my family moved from a small Amish settlement
in Gettysburg, Pennsylvania, to a farm outside of Shippensburg, Pennsylvania. This Amish community was twice the size of my previous
home, which for a girl of eleven was both exciting and scary. Adjusting
to a new school, meeting new schoolmates and a new teacher, attending
a new church, having new neighbors—so many good first impressions
to make.

One day shortly after we settled in, some English neighbors stopped
by to welcome us. As time went by, our friendship with them grew, and
we always looked forward to their next visit. We would all stop whatever
we were doing and sit around the kitchen table as Mom served coffee and
often her homemade shoofly pie. There are a lot of different recipes, but
my family's shoofly pie has a cakelike middle, a gooey molasses bottom,
and crumbs on top. When our English guests were present, we ate our pie
and drank our coffee separately, the way they did. But when non-Amish
guests weren't around, we soaked the shoofly pie with the coffee.

One day, after having lived at our new home for about a year, we were
having one of our coffee breaks with our neighbors when my younger
brother poured coffee over his shoofly pie. Children don't get a cup of

coffee as the adults do, but we always dribbled a few tablespoons of coffee onto our pie.

Our neighbor looked at my mother in shock and asked, "What is he doing?"

A little embarrassed, my mother explained that this was how some Amish people eat shoofly pie.

"Unbelievable," she exclaimed. Then she picked up her own mug of coffee and drenched her remaining pie. "I've been wanting to do this ever since our first coffee break, but I was afraid you'd think I was weird. I grew up eating my pie this way."

We get only one chance at making a good first impression. Being imperfect humans, we tend to be overly cautious, afraid of messing up. But when we're not our true selves, we can lose more than we gain.

Here's my mom's shoofly pie recipe.

MOM LEE'S SHOOFLY PIE

Pie crust:

3 cups all-purpose flour

2 tablespoons brown sugar

1 teaspoon salt

$1/4$ teaspoon baking powder

1 cup shortening (or two sticks of unsalted butter)

$1/4$ cup water (approximately)

Mix the dry ingredients—flour, brown sugar, salt, and baking powder. Cut the shortening or butter into the dry ingredients until crumbly. Add just enough water so you can roll out the dough using a rolling pin. Press into two or three 8" pie pans.

Filling:
2 eggs
3 cups brown sugar
2 cups Old Barrel molasses
1^1/$_2$ teaspoons baking soda
3 cups boiling water

Mix together, and pour into two or three unbaked 8"
pie shells, depending on the amount of filling used in
each pie.

Crumbs for the top:
1^1/$_2$ cups brown sugar
1 teaspoon baking soda
6 cups flour
^{1}/$_2$ teaspoon cream of tartar
^{1}/$_2$ cup Crisco
^{1}/$_2$ cup margarine or butter

Mix the dry ingredients, and then add the Crisco and
butter until the mixture is crumbly. Put the crumbs on
top of each pie, and bake at 400 degrees for 10
minutes. Then reduce the temperature to 350
degrees, and bake for another 45–50 minutes or
until done. Cool and serve.

From Cindy

My family was really hungry, but the plan for dinner was a simple
one—pasta salad and bread. It was summertime, and I'd been mom-the-
lifeguard at the local pool most of the day while my children swam with

friends. For supper I had made a pistachio pasta salad from a new recipe. I thought its pretty shade of green looked quite appetizing.

After my husband said the mealtime prayer, I poured milk into the children's glasses while they began to eat. Each one took a bite of the pasta, gagged, and spit it out in the napkin.

"Mom, that green stuff is the worst thing I've ever tasted." My oldest son, always bluntly honest.

His younger brother shrugged, not wanting to hurt my feelings. "I'm really not hungry after all."

My husband downed a glass of tea after he'd taken a bite. "I'm sorry, sweetie, but Justin's right."

Convinced it couldn't be that bad, I took a forkful. I too gagged and spit it out in my napkin. I have no idea what I did wrong to that recipe. I stood up and said, "Well, let's go."

I was met with looks of intrigue and hope. Not only was I going to spare them having to eat the awful meal, but we were going out to eat? They were in the car before I had time to grab the milk and put it in the refrigerator.

A few days later one of the boys was pushing me to get his way. I pointed at him and said, "Watch it, kid, or I'll make that green stuff again."

Frustration drained from his face. He held up his hands like stop signs. "No, please. I'll do anything not to have to see, smell, or eat that stuff!"

A humorous threat can be a great way to caution someone who's out of line and bring a smile at the same time. But more than that, it helps people be more comfortable in their own skin.

A Little Laughter Can Go a Long Way

All the days of the afflicted are evil: but he
that is of a merry heart hath a continual feast.

—Proverbs 15:15

From Miriam

When our boys were younger, our son Mervin and his cousin Stephen Esh, who is from the town of Lancaster, exchanged weeklong visits each summer. Whether the boys were bottle-feeding calves, swinging on long ropes in the loft of the hay barn, or shopping for school supplies, it was always twice the fun when done together. Stephen loved farm life, so we always sent him home with a gift from the farm—a pair of pigeons, rabbits, or baby kittens, all boxed up safely with holes for ventilation to give them plenty of air during the two-hour trip home.

One year when Stephen's parents came to pick him up, he presented his mother with the familiar cardboard box, which by now his mother had come to dread. "Oh please, no. Not another box with holes," she cried. "What is it this time?"

Slowly she opened the top flaps of the box, peeking inside and expecting to see some furry critter jump out at her at any minute.

Suddenly she burst into laughter and pulled out a brand-new pair of black and white canvas sneakers—our gift for the summer.

Like most people in all walks of life, the Amish love to laugh. One of the best gifts we give one another is our sense of humor. Laughter lifts our spirits and strengthens us. It even brings us hope, because once we've laughed, we can feel heaviness lift. Children laugh easily and often. Adults often bond through sharing lighthearted banter and laughter. Can you think of a way to make someone you love laugh today?

From Cindy

For a year after I attended my first writers' conference, I wrote for several hours each day between homeschooling our second grader, running the house, and keeping up with two active teenagers. I also dealt with some painful foot issues, and my podiatrist prescribed a year of corrective footwear with inserts. Those shoes were so ugly! But I obeyed the podiatrist's directions.

The day before I was to leave for my second writers' conference, I returned to the podiatrist for a routine visit. I was thrilled when he said I could start wearing any type of shoes I wanted to. I gleefully packed several pairs I hadn't been able to wear for a year.

The next afternoon my husband drove my rooming buddy and me to the airport, where we boarded a plane and flew to Houston. The following morning Vicki and I rose early to prepare for the long day of classes and talking with editors and agents.

Before jumping into the shower, I opened my suitcase and discovered I'd packed seven pairs of shoes and not one pair of underwear. The closest clothing store was more than thirty minutes away. If I went into town, I'd miss breakfast and my first class.

When I told Vicki what I'd done, she stared at me as if the words hadn't registered. How could a grown woman forget to pack underwear but bring every pair of heels she owned?

She went to her suitcase. "I picked up these at the last minute at the store the other night." She pulled out a package of brand-new underwear, ripped it open, and handed me a pair. I'd have to wash one of my two pairs of underwear each evening and hang them up to dry overnight, for four days. But at least I'd have clean underwear every day.

I told a couple of women at the conference about my mix-up, and one of them wrote my story on an index card and passed it to the emcee—without including my name. At the next group gathering, the emcee read it, creating quite a stir of laughter from the other attendees. Then she said if whoever belonged to that story would stand up, she could have a free book.

I argued with myself about whether to stand or remain silent. I stood. The laughter grew louder as this well-dressed woman with the soft voice and Southern accent took a red-faced bow before going up front to receive her free book.

Now, this story could be about making lists and being better organized, but it's not. If I made a list, I'd just lose it.

It could be about God's faithful provision in times of need, and that aspect shouldn't be overlooked.

But mostly it's about relaxing. I'm not perfect. Neither are you. We need to get over that expectation. I have areas where I shine. So do you. When we don't shine, we should relax and enjoy the ride.

The two women I told my story to became my critique partners. The tale came up at another conference I attended, though I didn't mention it, and because of that, writing doors opened. Who would've thought that my lack of packing skills could cause such a chain of events?

Um, perhaps God?

BEAUTY, ASHES, AND THINGS BETWEEN

SOMETHING ON THE SIDE: AMISH WOMEN AND THEIR COTTAGE INDUSTRIES

During one of my visits to Miriam's, we hitched a horse to a buggy, loaded up the children, and went to see some of her women friends and family. She asked what I called it when women had a small business in their home. I said, "A cottage industry." She said she called it "having something on the side." She added, "Almost every Amish woman has something on the side."

Stifling a chuckle, I explained to her that for the non-Amish, that term usually referred to a relationship outside of marriage. When she could close her mouth and take a breath again, she turned many shades of red and then burst into laughter.

Amish women carry out the traditional roles of wife and mother—keeping the home and raising children—but most also have a small business venture to help bring in money. The money an Amish woman earns goes toward meeting the needs of her family, just as a husband's money does, but both usually keep some of it to spend however they choose.

Our first stop was at the home of Miriam's *Mamm* (her mom). It was hot outside, but I felt more heat pouring through the screen door as we approached. Miriam's mother bakes a multitude of pies and pastries for several bakeries, some belonging to non-Amish people, some to the Amish. Besides the family kitchen, Miriam's mom has a separate room attached to her home where she bakes four days a week.

A stainless-steel gas oven with numerous shelves and doors stood five feet tall. Shelves on the walls held tall stacks of baking utensils. Long countertops were covered with uncooked piecrusts ready to be placed in a pan and filling added. A teenage girl stood at the sink, washing dishes.

Miriam's eight-year-old daughter put on an apron and began helping. She earns money helping out her *Mammi* (grandmother) during the summer. I couldn't believe Amanda wanted to spend a summer day inside a room with no air conditioning and ovens radiating heat. Amanda said she'd spent years waiting to be old enough to help make piecrusts. When she was younger, her job was washing dishes, sweeping, and getting the ingredients out of the pantry so her Mammi could keep baking.

After we visited for a few minutes, Miriam and I returned to our buggy. Along the "tour" route, we passed a woman with a roadside produce stand. A mile or so later, we saw an Amish woman getting out of her buggy at an Englischer woman's home. Miriam waved to her, then told me she cleaned people's homes for extra money. Other Amish wives bring in additional income by sewing quilts, working at a market, selling greenhouse-grown plants, or working once or twice a week in a restaurant.

Married Amish women don't hold full-time jobs. If a young woman has a job before she marries, she'll give up that job after marriage. However, there are two exceptions to that rule. If a couple can't have children or if all the children are grown and out of the home, the wife can fill her days in any manner she and her husband choose, including full-time work.

While raising children, women can run small businesses that fit around the family's schedule. Until we began writing together, Miriam had a craft business. It required long hours, but she often involved the whole family in making the items, and she was able to schedule her work hours around her family responsibilities...most of the time.

My home is filled with wall hangings and other crafts Miriam has made, and I love all of them. In addition to those items on display, I have several of her note cards. After her family helped her brainstorm ideas, she sketched several scenes on eight-by-ten-inch canvases and painted them. Then she took the originals to a graphics shop, where a man printed the images on four-by-five-inch note cards and provided the appropriate-size envelopes. Miriam and her family folded each one and placed small stacks of them in little boxes. She put them on consignment in various stores and sold them herself during craft shows. She sold crates of them to me, and I sold boxes of them through my Web site and gave them to people as thank-you gifts.

Single Amish women may work full-time in an Amish market or watch young children for an Englischer neighbor or teach school. Since wedding season is in the fall, schoolteachers know months before the school year starts whether they'll be able to teach that year or not. If a wedding is planned, a new teacher will be hired, usually a month or so before the first day of school.

Most single men and women live at home until they marry. While living at home and working a full- or part-time job, they usually give their parents some or all of the money to keep for them for later or to spend as needed for the family. Young men or women who have joined the faith but haven't married by the time they're in their middle twenties may choose to get a place of their own. Occasionally a few friends will rent a place together, but that's very unusual.

Few Amish women remain single, but I happen to be friends with one. She owns a very successful dry-goods store, and her parents' home is attached to hers so she can help take care of them. (She has several sisters who live nearby, and they also help with their parents.) She helps cater meals for weddings, travels throughout the United States on purchasing trips (with a hired female driver), and never has enough hours in the day for all she'd like to do. During one of my trips to Pennsylvania, she cooked a wedding feast for me so I could ask questions and take notes, and she also invited several Amish women. That whole evening is one of my most cherished memories. The next day I went to her store to discuss some book-related business, and she'd made me a Christmas salad.

Whenever I need a reminder of how to stay organized with a busy schedule, I spend a little time with her.

Her Christmas Salad is beautiful and absolutely delicious! So I asked if she'd send me the recipe.

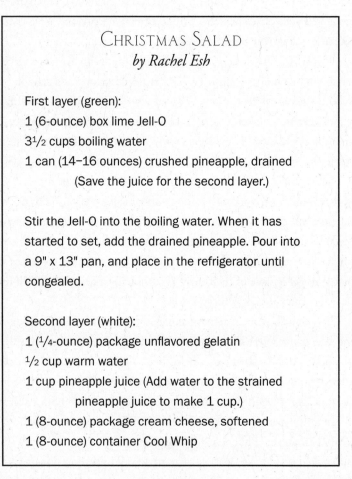

CHRISTMAS SALAD
by Rachel Esh

First layer (green):
1 (6-ounce) box lime Jell-O
3 1/2 cups boiling water
1 can (14–16 ounces) crushed pineapple, drained
        (Save the juice for the second layer.)

Stir the Jell-O into the boiling water. When it has started to set, add the drained pineapple. Pour into a 9" x 13" pan, and place in the refrigerator until congealed.

Second layer (white):
1 (1/4-ounce) package unflavored gelatin
1/2 cup warm water
1 cup pineapple juice (Add water to the strained
        pineapple juice to make 1 cup.)
1 (8-ounce) package cream cheese, softened
1 (8-ounce) container Cool Whip

Add the unflavored gelatin to $1/2$ cup of warm water, and stir until dissolved. Heat the pineapple juice until boiling. Stir in the gelatin mixture. Remove from the heat, and add the cream cheese. Let stand until completely cool, and then add the Cool Whip. When the first layer (green layer) is completely set, pour the second layer (white layer) over it.

Top layer (red):
1 (6-ounce) box strawberry or cherry Jell-O
$3^1/2$ cups boiling water

Stir the Jell-O into the boiling water. When it is completely cool and has started to set, add it to the top of the white layer. Chill until firm.

From Miriam

This is a handy dish I make for my family when I'm busy with my side business.

GREEN BEAN AND HAM CASSEROLE

$1^1/2$ cups shell macaroni
1 can green beans, drained
1 can condensed cream of mushroom soup, mixed
      with half a soup can of milk
1 to 2 cups cheddar cheese, grated (depending on
      how much cheese you like)

2 cups ham, chopped
1/2 cup onion, chopped
2 cups hash-brown potatoes, grated
salt and pepper to taste

Cook and drain the macaroni according to directions.
Layer ingredients, as listed, in a greased small
roasting pan or medium casserole dish. Bake at 350
degrees for 1 hour.

THE STING

Blessed are those who mourn, for they will be comforted.

—MATTHEW 5:4, NIV

From Cindy

First Corinthians 15:55 used to frustrate me. "O death, where is thy sting? O grave, where is thy victory?" Death has plenty of sting! Not for the believer who has died, but it sure hurts those who are left behind.

As I've matured, however, I've come to see the truth behind the painful reality of death.

In 2005 I belonged to an e-mail loop of about five hundred Christians, mostly aspiring authors. We were from all across the United States, and some were from other countries. One day a woman wrote, "Dear God, please don't make me watch my only child die."

When I read her e-mail, tears ran down my face. As I learned a little more about her, I found out that she lived in my area and that her son was a Marine. He had recently been diagnosed with cancer and was staying at a nearby hospital.

I bought a nice card and signed it from the group, gathered a few books she might enjoy reading while staying at the hospital, and went to visit her and her son. I didn't know what she looked like, but I knew what floor she'd be on. The nurses directed me from there.

When I arrived, the young man was having a procedure done. I found his mom in a waiting room, and we fell into each other's arms. The raw pain reflected in her eyes made me physically hurt, but I could see she was holding on to hope.

Her son's surgeon entered and invited me to visit the young man. That breach of standard protocol told me that he didn't have much time.

I prayed with him, asking God to help him feel encouraged by the love and concern the online group had for him and his parents. He assured me he had God's peace.

A few days later he died.

His parents mourned long and hard, but his mom told me that comfort surrounded her throughout every step of that journey. Healing their broken hearts came more slowly. Their grief will never completely cease, but I'm awed at the loving-kindness she exudes to everyone. She's an encourager who radiates God's love, and she willingly shares God's goodness through her writing.

She stopped writing fiction for a while but never stopped writing of His great love in her diaries. At the bottom of each e-mail, she has this paraphrase of Lamentations 3:22–23: "The Lord's mercies are new every morning; great is His faithfulness." As time passed, she began writing fiction again, and Connie's debut novel, *Leave Me Never,* was released a couple of months ago.[3]

From Miriam

In the fall of 2006, our community had to deal with the grief over the West Nickel Mines School shooting, in which five little girls were killed. The horror of it was thick in the air, and it showed on everyone's face, was heard in each conversation, and made daily headlines for weeks.

The tragedy took place a hundred miles west of our home, so it wasn't in our school district or church community, but three of my nephews were involved. Two were students in the school that day, and one worked as a volunteer fireman for a department that was dispatched to the school. So the pain and terror of that day stung our minds and hearts.

Nothing had ever shaken our world as fiercely as this did. As much as we tried to reassure our two school-age children (and ourselves), sending them to school each morning became harder instead of easier.

Amish school boards across the state met to discuss ways to make our children safer. After one such meeting, I left disappointed that the elders weren't doing more to protect the children and teachers in the local Amish and Mennonite schools.

I wrestled with frustration and fear. How could I help my children deal with their fear when I was struggling myself?

I remembered a window sticker I'd received about eight years earlier as a gift from *Guideposts* and had stuck on the glass of my front door. I went to the door and peeled off the sticker. Over the years the words had given my family and me a sense of security. Perhaps it could do the same for the children who attended our one-room schoolhouse.

Not sure how my two schoolchildren, Amanda and Mark, would feel about presenting the sticker to their teacher, I told them the original story. A would-be robber was armed with a gun and prepared to use it when he entered a store and threatened the owner. Then he read the sign above the door, which said, "God is our security guard, always on duty."

I asked if they wanted to take the sticker to school for their door. Their smiles put to rest any misgivings I had.

To this day that sticker reminds all the students in that schoolhouse who is really in control and gives them peace.

There is nothing wrong with providing some measures of protection for ourselves and our loved ones. But true peace can only be found by realizing that our only real shelter is God. We know the "thief" comes to destroy, but no matter what happens on this fallen planet, God knows how to heal the brokenhearted and how to give beauty for ashes (see John 10:10; Luke 4:18; and Isaiah 61:3).

When Life Gives You Scraps

Yet man is born unto trouble, as the sparks
fly upward.

—Job 5:7

From Cindy

My debut novels were a three-book series called Sisters of the Quilt. While writing those books, I learned some fascinating things about quilts.

Quilts provide a way for Amish women to be creative inside a restricted lifestyle. Sewing a quilt is also a great reason for the women to come together to accomplish a worthy goal. When my Amish friends make plans for an upcoming quilting, they talk about special creams for the coffee and delicious desserts. The fellowship involved in making a quilt helps to sew love, humor, and memories into each one.

A quilt is practical and adds beauty to any room, but it's so much more than that—both to the ones who sew it and to the ones who receive it. According to Amish tradition, when a couple marries, they receive two quilts as wedding gifts, one from each mom. Once a young woman tells her family she's expecting, someone close to her—perhaps her mom, grandmother, sisters, or aunts—begins working on a quilt in hopes of finishing it in time for the little one's birth. If the new parents name their baby after an Amish friend or relative, the woman of that household may make a quilt using fabric from clothes that belonged to the namesake when he or she was young.

The Amish often make quilts out of old fabric. The material may come from a grandmother's apron, a great-grandfather's homemade britches, a young woman's wedding dress, or even from the clothing of a child who died. One of my Amish friends, who is about my age, stored all her children's clothing in her attic and used those fabrics to make quilts for them as adults. She also collected (and still collects) old dresses, aprons, shirts, and pants from other family members.

Whatever the source, those precious scraps are used for patches, sashing, and the inside border of the quilt top. New fabric is used for the backing and often for the background of the quilt top.

A quilt like this becomes a journal of someone's past, captured by the fabrics used, fabrics passed down for generations.

I have a quilt that was sewn for me as a wedding present by a woman I call Mama Reh. I met Mama Reh when I was a teen, and on that day I learned that she was my biological grandmother (and that the woman I'd always thought was my grandma was actually my stepgrandmother).

Three decades later, that quilt still has the power to touch my heart. When I look at it, I see Mama Reh. Her effort to patchwork the pieces and sew them by hand, in spite of her rheumatoid arthritis, was her way of saying we are united by both seen and unseen threads.

I hadn't known how to properly care for a quilt, and it's in need of repair. So I have boxed it up, ready to take to an Amish friend who will use her expertise to fix it for me.

I will eventually pass this quilt down to my children. But it won't signify the humor and bonding that comes naturally in the Amish community. This quilt will represent something that ripped one generation from another, a reminder that relationships can be as fragile—and as easily broken—as the threads in a quilt. I hope it will help my family avoid making similar mistakes.

I don't know if I'll ever take up quilting, although several Amish friends have volunteered to teach me. But every one of us is sewing patchwork pieces of old and new cloth into the lives of our loved ones. Day after day we're making a quilt that we'll pass down to our children and grandchildren, one that is made of scraps from the lives of different people, events, and places. It's not as easily seen as a handmade quilt, and it may be tattered, but it's as beautiful and real as any other.

From Miriam

One winter evening our nephew Stephen Beiler was on horseback, returning home from a day's work. While still a mile or so away, his horse slipped and fell on a patch of hidden ice, resulting in a broken foot for the young husband and father of three.

With his foot in a cast, an already-tight budget and all the economic woes that go with it, and no ability to work, he could easily have become discouraged while on the mend. But instead of dwelling on doctors' bills and the money he wasn't making, Stephen focused on the good things he had going for him, taking the "scraps" from his injury and turning them into something else.

First, his injury could have been much worse; there was no costly hospital visit. Plus, being at home allowed him to do things with his family that his job had not permitted, like taking their second-grade daughter to school, spending more one-on-one time with his preschool-age son, and entertaining the baby while his wife did the housework. And one lazy afternoon as the children napped, he challenged his wife in a board game.

Instead of giving in to despair, Stephen and his family cherished their extra time together, making a quilt of memories. They trusted that God would, in His perfect time, heal the break. They also knew that this season would pass.

When life gives you scraps of frustration, disappointment, or worry… make your own quilt.

Having It All Together...or Not

As we have therefore opportunity, let us do
good unto all men, especially unto them who
are of the household of faith.

—Galatians 6:10

From Miriam

I have a red wooden sign hanging in my dining room that reads, "We
may not have it all together, but together we have it all."

Since our household doesn't always look like we have our act together,
these words give me peace. Having family around in an unbroken chain,
no single link missing, is among life's greatest blessings.

One weekend we had a couple visiting us who had lost not just one
but two sons in a tragic accident. As we sat around our table talking, I
heard the father whisper his wife's name, then caught a glimpse of him
nodding toward my red sign. A stab went through my heart. I couldn't
imagine what pain those words brought to them, the same words that
gave me peace. I wished I'd taken the sign down, but it was too late.

What comfort could I give them now? I finally concluded that even
though the whole family wasn't together now, while they had been
together, they had been very close-knit. They often took family vacations,
and they were always mindful of spending time with their boys. Their
teenage boys rarely went to bed without a hug and an "I love you" from

their father. How often do we take advantage of the opportunities right in front of us?

Surely the fact that they'd "had it together" with few regrets gives them peace of mind. And they have the comfort of knowing they will meet again, and then the links of the chain will be together—unbroken, complete, forever.

A Song
In Memory
BY AMANDA FLAUD

I hold my head in my hands,
As the tears roll down my face.
In my heart I'm feeling emotions rage.
Why did this have to happen?
I fall to my knees and pray.

And I know this isn't the end.
It won't be long till I see you again.
I will run through heaven's door.
I won't have to wait anymore.

When I look at God's amazing creation,
I can see that smile on your face.
And when I listen to beautiful worship music,
I can hear you laughing.
Your memory still lives on.

And I know this isn't the end.
It won't be long till I see you again.
I will run through heaven's door.
I won't have to wait anymore.

From Cindy

I was ten years old when my family traveled in a packed station wagon from Maryland to Alabama to visit relatives. At one point on the trip, we stopped at a wax museum. I was fascinated. I studied the images in the displays, reading about the lives of the people depicted by the statues.

As we approached the last display, my dad reminded us that it was almost time to pile into the car and hit the road again. I soaked in that display and then turned around to speak to my mom. But she wasn't there. I searched the crowded room. None of my family was there.

I stayed put, waiting for them to return. They didn't. As the minutes ticked by and the wall clock showed they'd been gone half an hour, and then forty-five minutes, I knew they were not just in the restroom or at a vending machine. They'd left without me.

An awful feeling took up residence in my gut. The room was filled with families, but none of them felt like a part of me. Until that moment I hadn't realized *family* had a feeling to it, but clearly it did—in spite of the arguments and frustrations with siblings and the "unfair" stances my parents took. As I waited and fear tap-danced on my emotions, I also began to understand the word *stranger* from a totally different point of view. My heart longed for the familiar, for the ones who knew me and cared about me. I sensed a chasm in my heart that separated me from everyone in that room.

Time ticked by, and the sick feeling in my gut increased.

Finally my mom and dad entered the last display area—security guards in tow. Relief flooded me, and instantly a sense of belonging replaced the sick feeling. Mom smiled casually, but her body trembled when she embraced me. Dad ruffled my hair and then pulled me into a hug.

Hoping I wouldn't get in trouble, I explained, "I was looking at a display, and when I turned around, you were gone."

Mom nodded. "I know." She put her arm around my shoulders. "I'd told you to come on, and I thought you heard me. I forgot that you don't hear anyone when you're studying something. I'm sorry. Your dad and I thought you'd jumped in the 'way back' and were lying down." The "way back" was what we called the cargo area of the station wagon, and during long trips I usually ran to the car ahead of everyone, jumped in the "way back," and lay down.

We walked through the packed building and out to the parking lot. My siblings hopped out of the car and gathered around me, patting my back, hugging me, and asking me if I was okay. This group wasn't just another family who'd stopped by the wax museum. They were *my* family.

My brother smiled. "If you thought Dad drove fast before, you should've seen him when he realized you weren't with us."

My dad placed his large hand on the back of my neck and rubbed it. "Well, we couldn't show up at your grandparents without you. How would we explain *that*?" Then he glanced at Mom and chuckled. "I tease about lots of things, but I'd go as far and as fast as needed to find and keep you. You know that."

We climbed into the car, and I thought about what Dad had said. He was right; I did know how much he and Mom and my sister and brothers cared. We were family—through the fun, tough, annoying, angering, and blessed times.

I just didn't know until that day what a strong sense of belonging came with the word *family*.

Nevertheless, I Believe

But without faith it is impossible to please
him: for he that cometh to God must believe
that he is, and that he is a rewarder of them
that diligently seek him.

—Hebrews 11:6

From Cindy

I love what I call the Nevertheless Principle. The conflict resolution in the
Sisters of the Quilt series is founded on that principle, which is, that no
matter where we find ourselves, we can say, "Nevertheless…God."

He *is* the answer.

He *has* the answer.

When what we believed would happen didn't, or what we thought
we understood about God seems to be wrong or not enough, *nevertheless,*
He is the same yesterday, today, and forever.

Nevertheless sets aside the differences among people in various divi-
sions of the Christian faith and enables us to focus on the only thing that
really matters: believing in the Father, Son, and Holy Spirit.

For those who believed for a miraculous healing but didn't receive
one, *nevertheless* offers strength and hope anyway.

For those who've experienced a tragedy that left them at odds with
everything and everyone, including God, *nevertheless* offers reconciliation
with Him.

We live on a fallen planet that we don't understand and can't accept much of the time. Nevertheless, God is on our side. He is for us and not against us. And whether or not we understand what's happening in our world or in the world around us, we can choose to say, "Nevertheless, God is my strength, as well as my yesterday, today, and tomorrow."

Life hurts. Nevertheless, it is a gift worth honoring.

Believing in *nevertheless* may seem childlike. But Matthew 18:4 tells us how Jesus felt about the humility of a child.

The Nevertheless Principle gives me peace. It offers me faith that reaches beyond my understanding, beyond my emotions, beyond my fears. *Nevertheless* says, "I don't have to understand; I believe anyway."

From Miriam

Losing a loved one can be devastating. Some people take years to overcome the loss. Some never fully recover. Yet death is as much a part of life as life itself.

Precious memories are the greatest inheritance anyone could leave behind. They can never be lost or stolen but can be recalled and cherished and shared for years.

In 2005 we lost a dear aunt to cancer. Acceptance didn't come easy. But trusting that she was with the Lord and reveling in our fond remembrances of her helped ease the pain. Aunt Becky was one of the most cheerful people I've ever known, naturally spreading sunshine and happiness to those around her.

Aunt Becky was also known for her delicious sweet dinner rolls, which she often made for church gatherings. They were a mouth-watering treat. She baked them in pie pans to a perfect golden brown and shaped them in a way that reminded me of honeycomb. They probably had a real name at one time, but to this day everyone in the family just calls them Aunt Becky's dinner rolls.

In the ever-changing seasons of life, death is inevitable. Since remembering the loved one's life can be such a comfort, it is important that we strive to make good memories while we're alive. That way we strengthen those who are left to deal with the grief. Nevertheless, we will meet again in eternity and experience Aunt Becky's warmth.

AUNT BECKY'S DINNER ROLLS

2 tablespoons yeast, dissolved in $1\frac{1}{2}$ cups warm water
4 cups warm water
$1\frac{1}{2}$ cups sugar
1 teaspoon salt
4 cups mashed potatoes
5 eggs, beaten
2 cups whole-wheat flour
1 cup cooking oil
6 cups bread flour

Dissolve yeast in $1\frac{1}{2}$ cups of warm water. Add the rest of the warm water (4 cups). Add the sugar and salt; mix well. Add the potatoes and eggs; mix well. Add the 2 cups of whole-wheat flour; mix well. Add oil; mix well. Add the bread flour. Knead well, cover, and set aside to rise. Knead well; let rise again. Shape into 2" balls, seven to a pie pan. Let rise slightly. Then bake at 350 degrees for 20–30 minutes. Makes approximately two dozen rolls.

Light in the Dark

For thou art my lamp, O LORD: and the
LORD will lighten my darkness.

—2 SAMUEL 22:29

From Miriam

As the sun was setting, Amanda was mowing the last few rounds of grass with the reel mower, determined to finish before dark. Seeing something unusual blinking in the grass, she stopped and bent down to pick it up. To her dismay she realized she had run over a firefly, and the reel mower had cut off part of its wing. Saddened, Amanda brought the lightning bug to me.

"Look, Mom," she said. "He just keeps on blinking. He's crippled, but his light keeps on shining."

I immediately thought of our English friend Gary, who twenty-some years ago was critically injured in a farming accident. He wasn't expected to live, but he survived. The doctor said he'd never walk again, but he's still walking today.

His life has certainly not been easy. He endures more pain in a month than most people do in a lifetime. Yet he rarely complains and will go the extra mile for anyone.

His circumstances would cause many people to give up on life and give up on God. But Gary continually blesses those around him. His light shines on in the midst of darkness.

From Cindy

I was almost fifteen when my family moved from Maryland to Alabama. Emotionally, we found it to be the hardest move we'd ever made. My dad was traveling more than ever, and my mom had severe allergies that showed up practically overnight—due to the region or the fixer-upper we'd bought or both. She had constant headaches, but she faced each day determined not to let them stop her from doing what needed to be done. There were just three of us kids by then because Kathy had married the year before we moved. We missed the friends we'd left behind and our sister, but we took our mom's lead and remained hopeful.

One day I noticed that my special-needs brother, Leston, had bled in the shower and on the bathroom floor. I told my mom, and she took him to the doctor, where the tests resulted in a confusing array of diagnoses. After a few weeks the team of doctors thought they'd identified the issue and so performed corrective surgery.

After the procedure Leston developed blood clots and had to be given blood thinner, but that caused him to seep a lot of blood from the incision area. Within days he was in ICU, fighting for his life.

For weeks my mom stayed at the hospital every night and came home each morning to get my brother Mark and me off to school. She then grabbed a shower, prepared after-school snacks, and headed back. My dad had to keep working, but when he wasn't traveling, he helped make dinners, pick up groceries, and do dishes. He also insisted that Mark and I focus at school and during homework time.

I was the typical youngest child, and suddenly I needed to carry responsibility and be proactively helpful. But I just wanted our old life back—the one we'd left in Maryland, where I had friends and an intact family.

Finally my brother began to get better, and when Mom came home with him, she wasn't the same woman who'd left. Leston might not survive, but even if he did, he faced long months of recuperation before he could bathe, dress, or get to the restroom on his own. Mom had always been strong and patient and had filled our home with constant humming. Now silence reigned. She had no smile. When the phone rang, she jolted. Her sense of humor had been stolen, and she easily raised her voice.

Leston wanted to eat, but he fought and fussed about the mandated diet of baby food. One day he and Mom argued so much she stormed out of his bedroom, slamming the door. He threw his food tray at the door. Mom stalked out of the house and to the shed. I'd seen her go there a few times that week, but this time I followed her.

She stood just inside the door, her face buried in her hands, weeping. I hugged her tight. My insides quaked with fear that if Leston didn't survive, neither would Mom.

We talked for several minutes. I questioned her stooping to his level and arguing with him. She agreed that I had a point and apologized for not handling herself better. I assured her that she didn't have to be perfect, that I would always love her, that we all would.

As we walked back to the house, she put her arm around my shoulders and thanked me. I hadn't done anything except let her know I cared. But somehow those few words, even though mixed with gentle correction from a teen, brought light and hope into her weary heart.

When we went into Leston's room, Mark had cleaned up the mess and was sitting on Leston's bed with two spoons in a fresh bowl of baby food.

Mark took a bite. "This isn't bad. You guys should try it."

Leston looked at Mom, picked up the other spoon, and ate a small mouthful of the baby food. "He's right. It's not that bad."

Some family arguments are necessary, and they can be the beginning of seeing another person's point of view. Arguing is often one person trying to get a message through to the other—one person's light trying to get past the darkened understanding of the other. The odd and beautiful thing is that each person caught in the argument may have a light that needs to penetrate the other's area of darkness.

Unexpected Refuge

God is our refuge and strength, a very
present help in trouble. Therefore will not
we fear, though the earth be removed, and
though the mountains be carried into the
midst of the sea.

—Psalm 46:1–2

From Miriam

Horse-drawn buggies lined the fence outside our one-room schoolhouse. Inside, dozens of paper snowflakes hung from the ceiling on seemingly invisible strings, swaying as cold gusts of air swept through the door each time another family arrived for the Christmas program.

Everyone settled into the students' chairs, and a hush fell over the room as nervous scholars began to perform. Seeing the innocent faces of children as they sang Christmas hymns, recited original poems, and acted out their play put the true holiday spirit in each person's heart.

When the performance ended and the teacher tapped the bell to dismiss everyone, the room went from order to chaos. As children lined up for refreshments, the parents visited. I was making a mental list of Christmas preparations that needed to be done the minute I got home when I noticed murmurs of shock spreading through the room. My husband sought me out and explained that my cousin's house was burning. The gas refrigerator had exploded. He told me to take the children home in the horse and buggy; he would head to the fire with the rest of the men.

Once at home I could think of little else but my cousin and her family of eight children. I had to be there. So I walked to the home of an English friend, Vanessa, and asked her to drive me.

Heavy smoke hung in the air. The land where my cousin's house had once stood was now a deep, black, smoldering pit. Choking back tears, I greeted some of the family who stood huddled together, watching.

Fire trucks and personnel were everywhere. Despite their best efforts, the house and all the family's belongings had gone up in flames or suffered irreparable water damage. But, thankfully, no one was hurt. The family had been at their own school program when the fire started.

Family, friends, and neighbors cleaned out the three-bay buggy shed (the Amish version of a three-car garage) to serve as temporary living quarters. A pickup arrived with beds. Someone delivered an RV for additional sleeping quarters.

The community spirit of service over the next four weeks was truly amazing. But what touched my heart even more was the help that came from our English neighbors and friends. A local lumber company gave the family huge discounts on many supplies for the new house and even donated some items. Credit accounts were set up at the bank and at Rachel's Country Store so people could donate funds for furniture, appliances, housewares, and material for new clothes. A local driver provided a month of free trips. Ladies from Mowersville Brethren in Christ Church provided meals for the carpenters. Schwan's delivered ice cream at no charge. Even the unopened Christmas gifts for the children were replaced, and many more came in time for the holidays.

Approximately twenty working days after the fire, the grateful family moved into their new, fully furnished, and stocked home.

I feel blessed to live in a community where there is such unity. And I hope that our simple way of life is not a burden to our English neighbors. I'd like to think that we are as much a blessing to them as they are to us.

As opportunities arise, we need to search for ways to help those in need, overlooking differences in color or culture and concentrating on what we have in common: the same heavenly Father.

From Cindy

My husband and I had known Dr. Mark Rutland for a long time, so when we learned that he'd founded a new ministry, we were excited to support something we knew we could trust.

Mark founded Global Servants[4] and through that ministry opened House of Grace, a home in Thailand for tribal girls at risk of being sold into sexual slavery by their families. The goal of House of Grace is to prevent girls from being sold, because rescuing them afterward is far more difficult.

When House of Grace began, Tommy and I couldn't give money, but we prayed for the girls and dreamed of someday becoming a sponsor. Sponsors provide redeeming love to save young girls from slavery. A destitute father or stepfather (or an uncle or a mother) who can find no other way to feed his family may sell a daughter, usually when she's between the ages of six and nine. Sometimes another relative—typically an aunt or grandmother—has compassion on the young girl and finds a way to get word to House of Grace.

From the beginning Mark felt that it would be wrong to pay the family for the girl in order to rescue her. Instead, House of Grace offers to take her in—feed her, house her, and pay for her to attend the local school. A representative assures the father or stepfather that his daughter will be able to bring the family more money in the long run if she's educated and can get a good, steady job. The father may spend several days wrestling with the decision, but a desire to do what's best for the child has always prevailed. To this point House of Grace has never been turned down.

It isn't an ideal solution. My heart would break if I had a daughter raised in a communal home rather than with loving parents. But it's the best alternative for these girls.

About twelve years ago Tommy and I became sponsors of a girl. Our little girl has grown into a young woman and will soon graduate from school and enter college. The joy of getting to be a part of this kind of ministry is hard to define. In a country where supporting our local churches seems like a drop of water in an ocean, having the opportunity to make a tangible difference in someone's life feels like salve to a weary heart. I hope our foster daughter and all those who have been sponsored by House of Grace are able to accept with peace and grace that what we've offered them is far from perfect. It's imperfect perfection—better than what would have been but not anything like what God wants to do as they continue their journey on this planet.

I pray that we too can take our eyes off the imperfect situations that have molded our lives and instead focus on the difference God has made and will continue to make.

In His
Hands

SIMPLE
CELEBRATIONS

The Amish celebrate Christmas, Easter, Thanksgiving, and birth-days with simplicity and tradition.

Easter may include fixing a basket of candy and coloring eggs and hiding them for the children, but the celebration doesn't include the Easter bunny.

Birthdays are most often celebrated at home around the table with simple gifts, a homemade cake, and favorite songs after the evening meal. Sometimes the older teens and adults plan silly surprises for one another—like gathering friends and relatives and hiding them in a barn or small bedroom to surprise the birthday person, or waking the birthday person early in the morning to see a group of friends or relatives crowded into the bedroom to sing to the sleepy honoree. The Amish ways are structured, but they allow a lot of room for fun and laughter.

For Thanksgiving the men often bring home wild turkeys to pluck and cook. I've been at Miriam's home when all the men went hunting. It's a special time of fellowship for everyone—the men who go off hunting together and the women who have a day or two on their own to visit one another. Let me tell you, turkey from the grocery store's freezer is nothing like a freshly prepared and cooked turkey. When I took my first bite, it was as if I'd never tasted turkey before in my life.

Christmastime is very special for the Amish. The parents look forward to the cute skits the schoolchildren will perform inside the one-room schoolhouse. Amish children don't get a lengthy Christmas break like public school children. They get off for only two days, possibly two and a half. Amish schools may not close for half a day on Christmas Eve, but they are always closed on Christmas Day and the day following, called *Zwedde Grischtdaag*—Second Christmas. Many Amish look forward to Zwedde Grischtdaag as much as, if not more than, Christmas Day, because it's a special time for visiting friends and relatives.

When I first heard that, I thought, *You visit these people all the time.* But the main focus of regular visits is accomplishing work. Even church Sundays require a good bit of effort as they set up a home to seat and feed several hundred people. But Second Christmas is for kicking back and soaking in the power of Christ's birth. There is no to-do list—just long hours of chatting while eating leftovers and watching the children play with their new toys.

The Amish Christmas doesn't include Santa Claus, electric lights, tinsel, or decorated trees. They honor the season of Christ's birth in simple and creative ways.

We too can make holiday celebrations more memorable by keeping them simple. Here are several ideas inspired by the Amish way of celebrating Christmas:

- Turn off the lights. Light candles (or even pull out old kerosene lamps), and set the mood for an evening of singing carols, telling favorite family tales, or reading Christmas stories with friends and family.
- Put away the tinsel and expensive decorations. Pull out old Christmas cards and string them along the walls in your living areas. Spend a moment thinking about each sender.
- Keep gifts practical. Think of "tools of the trade," useful gifts that reflect what family members do in their respective professions.

- Consider making gifts for others. Homemade gifts are always appreciated for their personal touch.
- Show kindness to your neighbors. Bring your family and friends together to donate food, toys, and clothes to friends and neighbors who've been especially affected by the economy.
- Make the kitchen a haven. Prepare food in advance whenever you can so the day of festivities can be spent with loved ones. Don't get crushed by the stress and expense of doing it all yourself. Invite guests to bring their favorite traditional dishes.
- Make cleanup a family affair. When it's time, bring your family together in the kitchen. Talk about your favorite parts of the party while doing the dishes and wiping off counters.
- Be thankful. Giving thanks doesn't have to end with Thanksgiving. Spend time telling loved ones how much they mean to you throughout the season, and see how much joy it brings them…and you.

From Miriam

In the midst of a holiday, it's always helpful to be able to prepare the breakfast entrée the night before. Here's one that we often use when we have overnight guests.

Overnight Blueberry French Toast

12 slices bread, cut into 1" cubes
8 ounces cream cheese, cut into 3/4" cubes
1 1/2 cups fresh or frozen blueberries (or if canned,
          drained)
12 eggs
1/3 cup maple syrup
2 cups milk

Place half the bread cubes in a buttered 9" x 13"
baking dish. Top with cream-cheese cubes, blueberries, and remaining bread. Beat eggs, syrup, and
milk, and pour evenly over the bread. Cover with foil
and refrigerate overnight. Preheat the oven to 350
degrees. Bake, covered with foil, for 30 minutes.
Remove the foil, and bake for another 10–15 minutes
until the top is golden brown.

In the Garden

But I will sing of thy power; yea, I will sing
aloud of thy mercy in the morning: for thou
hast been my defence and refuge in the day
of my trouble.

—Psalm 59:16

From Cindy

My sister, Kathy, has a gorgeous singing voice. Even as a teenager, she
sang at weddings, had the lead in school plays, and belted out beautiful
tunes at county fairs. I longed to be able to sing. She kept assuring me I'd
get there one day. I earnestly prayed to be able to sing. At sixteen, when I
was home alone one day, I knelt beside the kitchen table and asked God
to give me a voice. When I rose, I tested my voice and discovered it hadn't
arrived yet. Maybe it took time for that kind of a request.

I tested my voice numerous times over the next few months, but I
never received a singing voice. However, at forty years old I discovered a
different type of voice—a writing one. Like singers, each author has a
distinct voice. When looking for a new author, editors and agents want to
find one with a distinct voice. Although a writing voice is harder to
explain than a singing voice, it's part of what sets one author apart from
another. In part it's about how that author's storytelling rhythm and beat
sounds to the reader.

Our strongest desires come from deep within, but our minds can't
always grasp what the true desire is. I had a heart's desire for a voice that
could touch others. I never once thought it might be something other
than a singing voice.

When we pray, we often express a deep desire. If we stop expecting a specific response, we may find the answer. And our voice, whether we're singing, writing, or speaking, is how we communicate to God and how we share God with others.

From Miriam

In our one-room schoolhouse, we start each day with devotions and singing. Our teacher taught us to enjoy singing, but as a ten-year-old I never looked forward to starting a song. So when it was my turn to lead the singing, I always chose the same song, one I was sure I could lead without stalling: "In the Garden." If my teacher grew tired of me choosing that song week after week, she never showed it.

Thirty-five years later, with a husband and six children of my own, I start my summer days in the garden. My garden, which provides fresh vegetables for my family, is also my little getaway.

With the dawning of a new day, garden hoe in hand, I slip outside for some quiet time among the corn, potatoes, tomatoes, and, of course, weeds. The weeds keep the area private, because the children have learned that an interruption could land them an unwanted job out here. So this is where I meditate.

On one particular morning, with a heavy heart regarding a certain issue in my life, I poured my heart out to God, begging Him for deliverance. I felt His presence, accompanied by a calming peace. With that peace came the memory of a song—my special song from long ago. As I sang, the words had a new meaning that touched my heart and brought tears to my eyes.

In the Garden

I come to the garden alone,
While the dew is still on the roses,

And the voice I hear falling on my ear
The Son of God discloses.

He speaks, and the sound of His voice
Is so sweet the birds hush their singing,
And the melody that He gave to me
Within my heart is ringing.

I'd stay in the garden with Him,
Though the night around me be falling,
But He bids me go; through the voice of woe
His voice to me is calling.

Chorus:
And He walks with me, and He talks with me,
And He tells me I am His own;
And the joy we share as we tarry there,
None other has ever known.[5]

I love my garden because it's not just a place where vegetables grow. It's where God meets with me on a personal, individual level.

If you invite Him, God will visit you anywhere. You don't need a garden or even a yard. Any spot will work, even the bathroom if that's the only private space you have. Light a candle and talk to God. He's amazing.

Mothers and Children

Now our Lord Jesus Christ himself, and
God, even our Father, which hath loved us,
and hath given us everlasting consolation
and good hope through grace, comfort your
hearts, and stablish you in every good word
and work.

—2 Thessalonians 2:16–17

From Cindy

No matter what was taking place in my life, I'd never been buried under anxiety. But when our oldest son got his driver's license and left the house on his own that first time, fears assailed me like a hurricane hitting the shore of an unprepared town. Had I spent a lifetime raising him just to lose him as he was about to launch into a life of his own?

I smiled and waved as he drove away, saying yet one more prayer over him for safety before I went into my home. I tried to focus on other things, but my insides quaked, not just for this outing, but for all the others ahead of me. Within two years our second son would have his license too. The gale force winds of fear battered me, and I felt powerless to stop them.

As the evening wore on, I grew angry at myself. Worrying was ridiculous. Would my anxiety prevent an accident or keep my son safe? Yet I felt powerless to tame the storm raging inside me.

That's when a twist of an old motto formed in my mind. If practice makes perfect, I didn't want to practice worrying!

Every time a bad image came into my thoughts, I decided that I'd imagine myself throwing it to the ground and then snatching up a worthy thought. Whenever fear started whispering, I'd mentally shout back, *Shut up!* Then I'd refocus my thoughts.

At first I failed miserably at convincing myself not to worry. But having a teenager who drives gives a mother lots of practice time.

When school functions kept Justin out after midnight, I made myself go to bed at my usual time. While lying there, I had to pull my thoughts away from the realm of fear, over and over. When I did doze off, I'd jerk awake, longing to know if my son was home, but I refused to get up and look in his room. I felt like a horrible mother. But I stayed in bed, late night after late night. When I'd wake the next morning, my mind would scream, *Go look! Make sure he got home.* Instead, I fixed a pot of coffee, poured myself a cup, had my Bible and prayer time, and began my workday. When Justin came to the door of my home office, I'd bid him a good morning as if I'd never doubted he was home.

I went round after round with anxiety for several months. But I would not become its slave. It wouldn't tell me what to do. I'd tell it.

If practice makes perfect, refuse to practice worrying.

From Miriam

The bedroom curtains swayed in the cool breeze at the end of another busy day. The clock ticked loudly as I pondered the day's events. Sleep would be long in coming.

At that moment my husband and our six children were scattered across four states, and my weary mind was having a hard time keeping track of everyone. Daniel and two of our sons—Jacob, twenty-five, and Mark, eleven—were in Massachusetts on a job. Our oldest son, David Alan, twenty-seven, and his young family were visiting in Indiana. Two more sons—Mervin, twenty-one, and Michael, twenty—were in Wyoming, working on separate ranches. That left only Jacob's wife and small son, our daughter, Amanda, and me at home in Pennsylvania.

I had just spoken to each of them on the phone. Except for Michael, whom I hadn't heard from in a week. With growing concern I tried to envision where he might be. He had talked about going to cow camp, where men herd cattle by horseback for miles to reach better grazing, camping out under the stars and in thunderstorms, among mountain lions and other wildlife. I tried not to worry but was not succeeding.

If only I could talk to him, maybe I could relax. But they didn't have phone service in that remote area. So I worried…and prayed…and prayed some more.

I couldn't be everywhere or do everything. But God could. I couldn't reach my son by phone. But I could reach God through prayer. The thought that God could see my son at that very moment brought me peace.

I imagined God looking down on my son as the guys sat around the campfire looking up at the same moon that gave my darkened bedroom a comforting glow. A peaceful feeling washed over me, and trusting that He would watch over Michael, I fell into a restful sleep.

Blessings

BY AMANDA FLAUD

Praise God…
> For the opportunity to start over at the dawn of each
> new day.

Ask God…
> To use you for a lamp so He can shine through you.

Thank God…
> For giving you another awesome day with the people
> you care about.

GRATEFULNESS

Praise the LORD. Give thanks to the LORD,
for he is good; his love endures forever.

—PSALM 106:1, NIV

From Cindy

When I was a child, my mom or dad put the food on my plate, and all of it had to be eaten before I could leave the table. I gagged my way through many a meal, was sent to my room during mealtime, and often ended up sitting at the table by myself while everyone else went to watch television. The upside is that I learned to eat foods I didn't like. The downside is that I still hate most of those same foods.

As a result of my experiences, when my children said they hated something after trying it, I gave them a choice of other items with similar nutritional value. One son disliked most fresh fruits, but he loved certain ones and almost all fruit juices—100 percent pineapple, orange, apple. He hated cooked carrots, broccoli, and English peas but would eat raw carrots and broccoli. He still doesn't eat English peas.

Was my method helpful, or did I teach my children to expect to like what's placed in front of them? Was my parents' method better in the long run?

I don't know.

But I do know that no parents are as right as they hope to be at the time the decisions are made. Our one redeeming grace for all the verdicts we must give—and the fruit they bear—is that God is fully capable of redeeming our children from our brilliance. First Peter 1:3–4 says,

"According to his abundant mercy [God] hath begotten us again unto a lively hope by the resurrection of Jesus Christ from the dead, to an inheritance incorruptible, and undefiled, and that fadeth not away, reserved in heaven for you."

For that, we can all be extremely grateful.

From Miriam

The *clip, clop, clip, clop* of the horses' hoofs pounded in perfect rhythm on the asphalt as my daughter and I drove slowly toward home. My day had started long before the sun rose. I had washed and hung laundry on the clothesline to dry, got Mark, my eleven-year-old, off to school, picked ten to fifteen dozen ears of sweet corn and loaded them onto our horse-drawn wagon to take to my sister's—all before eight o'clock. After spending all day husking, washing, blanching, and then cutting the corn off the cobs and bagging it to freeze, Amanda and I were finally on our way home.

I had been tempted to call for a driver to take us that morning since we had such a busy day ahead of us. But as we drove home along the country road in the late-summer sunshine, I found the slow buggy ride enjoyable.

Being Amish isn't always easy. Sometimes our rules and guidelines make life a little harder than I'd like. Yet doing without holds blessings too.

If I had a car, I'd whiz around in all my busyness instead of enjoying the slow pace of a relaxing buggy ride on a beautiful afternoon.

As much as I would like to use a dryer during bad weather, I'd miss the pleasure that comes from taking a basketful of clothes into the fresh morning air.

A microwave oven must be handy, but I'd never want to be without my faithful old wood-burning cookstove. I light a fire in it on cool autumn mornings to take the chill off my kitchen as my family gathers for breakfast. I love the faint smell of wood smoke, and the crackle and pop of the fire is music on a cold day.

The hot days of summer can be trying. But since I don't have an air conditioner, I try to work outdoors in the garden or yard in the coolest hours and stay inside where my brick home keeps me reasonably cool during the hottest part of the day. I open the windows and listen to the birds on bright sunny days, the gentle rains on cloudy days, and the sound of horses passing by my home. Open windows make it easier to hear the ringing of my telephone from the outdoor phone shanty, and that keeps me from missing important calls from one of my children or a sister or friend who needs to chat.

Leaving it all in God's hands, I thank Him for the challenges as well as the blessings.

SEEKING AND FINDING

And we know that all things work together
for good to them that love God, to them who
are the called according to his purpose.

—ROMANS 8:28

From Cindy

A few months ago I was by myself in unfamiliar territory, driving from one author event to another. My vehicle has a GPS system, which is great, but it isn't much help without an address. So I pulled off the road, dug my BlackBerry out of my satchel, and looked for the address of the radio station where I was scheduled to give an interview. I quickly realized I hadn't logged that into my list of contacts.

Then I remembered I'd received the info via an e-mail a few weeks back. I scrolled through my recent e-mails. Within two minutes I found what I was looking for. My laptop sat on the passenger seat next to me, so I opened it and jotted down notes I needed to think about before arriving, and I listed the phone number as well. I then turned off my XM radio, called the radio station, and asked for their street address. After ending the call, I put their address in my GPS, punched the reroute button, turned my XM station back on, and headed for the new destination.

As I drove, I thought that just fifteen years ago I didn't own a cell phone. I never traveled by myself. I spent my days homeschooling my children, tending to the wood stove in winter, and folding mounds of cloth diapers.

Life never stops changing, even for the Amish. Fortunately, our God is the same yesterday, today, and forever, and yet He knows how to help us navigate every change we'll encounter.

From Miriam

WHEN I SAY, "I AM A CHRISTIAN"
BY CAROL WIMMER

When I say, "I am a Christian"
I'm not shouting, "I've been saved!"
I'm whispering, "I get lost!
That's why I chose this way"

When I say, "I am a Christian"
I don't speak with human pride
I'm confessing that I stumble—
needing God to be my guide

When I say, "I am a Christian"
I'm not trying to be strong
I'm professing that I'm weak
and pray for strength to carry on

When I say, "I am a Christian"
I'm not bragging of success
I'm admitting that I've failed
and cannot ever pay the debt

When I say, "I am a Christian"
I don't think I know it all
I submit to my confusion
asking humbly to be taught

When I say, "I am a Christian"
I'm not claiming to be perfect
My flaws are all too visible
but God believes I'm worth it

When I say, "I am a Christian"
I still feel the sting of pain
I have my share of heartache
which is why I seek His name

When I say, "I am a Christian"
I do not wish to judge
I have no authority
I only know I'm loved[6]

Giving and Accepting

Give, and it shall be given unto you; good measure, pressed down, and shaken together, and running over, shall men give into your bosom.

—Luke 6:38

From Cindy

When I heard about a stranger's set of circumstances, I longed to do something to help her. The woman, who spoke no English, had come to America to help her dying sister. After landing at the airport, the woman attempted to hire a taxi, but as soon as all her belongings, including her purse, were loaded, the alleged taxi driver drove off.

Tommy and I had no extra money to speak of. The few hundred dollars we did have was for that month's mortgage payment. But our lack of funds didn't ease my feeling that I should do something for this woman. So I cleaned out our storage room, closet, drawers, and cabinets, put a price tag on each item, and had a yard sale, which brought in nearly a hundred and fifty dollars.

I'd heard that an offering plate would be passed for her during a church service on the other side of town. I knew people with money would easily give a lot more than my paltry amount, but I had to follow my heart. I passed the money to her anonymously. I never even met the woman.

It wasn't much, but it was all I had to give. And I had to trust that whatever that money couldn't accomplish wasn't my responsibility. I'd done my part, and I trusted that God would do His.

From Miriam

My sister Sarah became a grandmother for the first time at the age of forty. As she sat in the hickory rocker by the stove, gently rocking her newborn granddaughter, her joy knew no bounds. She held the pink bundle close to her heart as memories of her own firstborn replayed in her mind.

Ruthie, the new mom, brought out her own baby book. As Sarah turned the pages, she recognized her handwriting from years ago where she had filled in Ruthie's weight, length, color of eyes and hair, and all the memorable firsts. Sarah also noticed that her daughter had filled in some blanks on her own.

When the book asked for one of the child's fondest memories of a vacation, Sarah expected her daughter to have written about their trip to the beach in South Carolina or the week they spent on the coast of Maine touring lighthouses. But to Sarah's surprise, Ruthie had written that the best vacations were the ones at home on the farm, when her mother packed a picnic lunch and took the kids down to the creek behind the barn. She and her brothers spent many a lazy afternoon wading in the water or riding the low-hanging branch of an uprooted tree that hung over the creek, pretending it was a horse. Then they would all sit under the shade tree and enjoy their picnic.

Tears blurred Sarah's vision as she swallowed the lump in her throat. She had always leaned toward the simple things in life. Money was usually tight for the young farming family, but by giving what she could, Sarah gave her children one of the most important things a mother can give—*time*.

It touched her heart to know that her married daughter also treasured the simple things, remembering that time with family is important, no matter where it's spent.

INNOCENCE
IN ACTION

> Brethren, I count not myself to have
> apprehended: but this one thing I do,
> forgetting those things which are behind,
> and reaching forth unto those things which
> are before.
>
> —PHILIPPIANS 3:13

From Miriam

As a five-year-old, my brother Johnny loved playing in the family carriage while it was parked…without the horse hitched up, of course. His imagination could take him for miles. Unfortunately, this sport was strictly forbidden by our father.

One afternoon *Daed* came home from work earlier than usual and found Johnny playing in the forbidden carriage. Sticking his head in the door, Daed asked, "Son, why are you playing in the buggy when I've told you not to?"

His startled son replied, "Because…I didn't know you were at home."

In the face of such innocent honesty, Daed couldn't keep a straight face.

I wonder how many times we adults try the same antic as that five-year-old. When we think our "Daed" isn't looking, we do things we know aren't right. But the Scriptures tell us that we can be sure our sins will find us out (see Numbers 32:23). I don't want to be caught doing something the Lord has told me not to, especially since I know that His rules are for my own good.

From Cindy

We all believe lies about ourselves at one time or another. You may know the lie you believe. Or your behavior might indicate that you believe a lie you don't even realize you've accepted.

Most books—whether inspirational, secular historicals, women's fiction, romance, suspense, or mystery—are built around one principle: what lie the characters believe about themselves.

One of my early childhood memories is of my mother reading to me before bedtime. For me, bedtime came really early. In spring and summer, the sun shone for a long time after I had to crawl into bed. I could hear other children playing in nearby yards and often wondered why I had to go to bed so much earlier than other five-, six-, and seven-year-olds. My conclusion was that I was such a pain that my family could only get relief by banning me to a room by myself.

I now know there were good reasons for my mom putting me to bed early during those years. She had health issues, including back problems. My dad left for work around four in the morning and returned home around five at night. The six of us had dinner together as a family, watched a television show, and then it was time for me, as the youngest, to go to bed.

How many times do we make something personal when it wasn't about us at all?

Another lie we buy into comes from comparing our weakest area with someone else's strongest area, to the point we start believing that we're not any good at anything. We think of our uniqueness as oddness. Because we haven't yet found where we fit, we decide we don't fit anywhere.

The problem with lies is that there's always a smidgen of truth inside them. Our challenge is to disbelieve the lies, and if we can't do that, we must choose to believe God more than we believe the lies. I've found several Bible verses that help me stand against the lies that assail me. One of my favorites is Philippians 1:6: "Being confident of this, that he who began a good work in you will carry it on to completion until the day of Christ Jesus" (NIV). Another helpful verse is 2 Corinthians 10:12: "But they measuring themselves by themselves, and comparing themselves among themselves, are not wise."

What lie do you believe about yourself? How will you combat that lie and begin to believe what God says about you instead?

SWIMMING UPSTREAM

For all these have of their abundance cast
in unto the offerings of God: but she of her
penury hath cast in all the living that she
had.

—LUKE 21:4

From Miriam

Many times I've questioned certain things or desperately wanted an answer on a particular subject—an instant answer if possible. I wish I could ask God a question and have Him answer right back.

I enjoy almost all reading, but I've never been fond of reading instructions. I've attempted to put grills, strollers, highchairs, and even a swing set together without studying the manuals first. I'd rather bake from memory than bother with a cookbook. Only when all else fails do I finally give in and get out the much-needed directions.

Then one day I came across 2 Timothy 3:16: "All scripture is given by inspiration of God, and is profitable for doctrine, for reproof, for correction, for instruction in righteousness." Those words reminded me of how stubborn I am with assembly instructions. But I also realized that I was the same way with some spiritual matters.

Since the authors of the Bible were inspired by God Himself, Scripture is the next best thing to having a one-on-one talk with Him. The Bible is our instruction manual for life.

Realizing my challenge with instructions and the "head knowledge" I gain when I read them, I had fresh incentive to read and study the Bible for "heart knowledge."

From Cindy

I love writing. I love spending long days and nights in my home office with the window open and research books all around me.

I'm an introvert, and I've heard that most fiction writers are. Being introverted is not the same as being shy, although shy people are often introverted. An introvert draws strength from quietness and solitude. An extrovert draws strength from get-togethers and other people-oriented events.

The first time I realized how much of an introvert I am, I was seventeen and on a first date. I had taken the time to straighten my long hair and do my nails and makeup and had even bought an especially nice-looking outfit. Our plan was to meet up with a group of friends at someone's home and have pizza. When my date asked if we could go to a drive-through for dinner instead, I felt tremendous relief wash over me.

Prior to that I'd often avoided going out, usually with the excuse that I wasn't "pulled together" enough. But at that moment it became clear to me that even at my best, I preferred quiet seclusion. I was a true introvert.

After going to the drive-through, my date and I went for a long, quiet stroll in a nearby park and tossed breadcrumbs to the ducks. The only way I would have enjoyed that night more was if I'd been alone with a pen and a journal.

So writing sounds like a good career choice for me, right?

Yet after my books appeared on several bestseller lists, I found myself thrust in front of cameras and microphones, including some national media. If that wasn't enough against my natural grain, I felt I should accept some of the invitations to speak at churches.

At this point you should feel sorry for my husband, who loves my quiet temperament, especially during football and baseball season. But if

I can't sleep because of an upcoming interview or speaking engagement, or if I'm walking around mumbling to myself because I'm displeased with how an interview went, he's the one who has to deal with my angst and try to help me through it.

Whether you're introverted or extroverted, being challenged is part of life. Following God wherever He leads is the only path to true success. How we look, feel, or sound while following Him has nothing at all to do with success. All He asks is that we follow as He leads and leave the results up to Him.

THE SHAPE
OF TOMORROW

The Daadi Haus (the Grandfather House)

My youngest son and I had visited the Flauds several times before my husband went with us. I knew Miriam's husband and mine would have a lot to talk about. In spite of their numerous differences, Daniel and Tommy have a good bit in common—both know about construction, farming, and raising sons.

Daniel's family trade is timber framing, an intricate skill of taking square timbers and building a frame in a way that supports an entire building without nails, bolts, or screws. Instead, wooden pegs are driven into tightly fitted joints. This is part of the Old Ways the Amish fathers have passed on to their apprenticing sons for generations, begun before nails, screws, and bolts were easily accessible and affordable through mass production. Timber framing is used for houses, barns, and even modern office buildings. It's been said that timber framing is as strong as a steel structure.

For the Amish, getting older means more honor and less work. Daniel's father now lives in a Daadi Haus (grandfather house) next to Daniel and Miriam. A Daadi Haus may be attached to the main house belonging to one of the adult children, or it may be a small home near the main house. A grandfather house is usually much smaller than the home the couple had when they were raising children, which makes it easier to clean.

Many Daadi Hauses have been passed down for generations. If there's not one already in the family, then after the children have families of their own, they build separate living quarters for the grandparents. The homes usually have kitchens so the grandparents can prepare their own food. The grandparents are close enough to join the others for a family meal, but they enjoy running their home and preparing their own meals.

The Amish appreciate the need for families to have their own space, but the elderly are highly respected, and they ease into retirement by carrying less responsibility without giving up all work-related duties. Some Amish never retire. They simply have a shorter workday. When an aging parent needs help, the younger generation lives close enough to lend a hand while tending to their own families.

Regardless of how some feel about living such a unique life, the wisdom and grit to change only when necessary—and never for the sake of convenience, entertainment, or ease of living—has equipped the Plain people to hold on to a lifestyle they believe in. Generation after generation, young people have decided to keep the Old Ways. While Englischers sit in classrooms through high school and sometimes college, young Amish men and women are working as full-time apprentices for employers who try to avoid ever having to lay them off or fire them. They remain focused on family, working in or taking over the family business, starting a family of their own, and eventually moving into a Daadi Haus of their own.

From Miriam

My mother-in-law and father-in-law live in the Daadi Haus next to us. I can prepare this simple recipe for them while cooking a meal for my family, or Mammi (pronounced "mommy") Flaud can easily fix this for the two of them.

SCALLOPED POTATOES
FOR TWO

2 potatoes, cooked and sliced
1 tablespoon butter
1 tablespoon flour
1 cup milk
1 teaspoon sour cream
$1/4$ cup chopped onion
$1/4$ cup chopped green pepper
1 teaspoon onion powder
dash each of salt, pepper, garlic powder, and
              parsley
Velveeta or cheddar cheese

Preheat oven to 350 degrees. Put the potatoes in
a small, greased casserole dish. Melt the butter
in a saucepan over low heat; stir in the flour, add
milk, and cook, stirring until thick. Add the sour
cream and stir. Add the onion, green pepper, and
seasonings. Pour the sauce over the potatoes,
and top with cheese. Bake uncovered for 30
minutes.

The recipe on the following page is often used if older parents haven't
been eating much but need some sustenance. I take this same recipe to
new moms; it's delicious and high in protein.

Egg Custard

4 cups milk
8 eggs, beaten
1/4 teaspoon salt
1 cup sugar
2 teaspoons vanilla
1 tablespoon cornstarch
1/4 cup cold milk
cinnamon

Heat 4 cups of milk almost to boiling. Mix together the eggs, salt, sugar, and vanilla; stir this mixture into the almost-boiling milk. In a small bowl, mix together the cornstarch and cold milk to make a runny paste; stir into the milk and egg mixture. Pour into a glass baking dish, and sprinkle with cinnamon.

Place the glass dish in a shallow baking pan, and add water to halfway up the side of the glass dish. Bake at 325 degrees for 1 hour or until custard seems firm.

LOOKING FOR ANSWERS

For whatsoever things were written aforetime
were written for our learning, that we through
patience and comfort of the scriptures might
have hope.

—ROMANS 15:4

From Miriam

The clock ticked loudly as I sat in our one-room school, observing the class. The students worked quietly as the teacher juggled all eight grades at once.

I had just served them all a hot lunch. The mothers had been taking turns bringing in hot meals once a week during January, February, and March to help ward off the winter blues. We did this as much for the teacher as for the children.

As I settled into my chair for an hour of relaxation, the teacher brought me her guest book, a large spiral notebook that all visitors were asked to sign. It was filled with artwork done by the students along with an introduction sheet for each child, describing who their parents, grandparents, and siblings were, their favorite subjects, and their favorite foods. The book also revealed what the students wanted to be when they grew up. One boy planned to be a fireman, another a policeman. Most wanted to be farmers or carpenters like their dads.

Most of the girls wanted to be teachers. A few hoped to tend a market stand. One little girl wrote that all she wanted to do was be a mother. That caught me off guard. Tears blurred my vision as I remembered something I'd read once:

> The most important occupation on earth for a woman is to
> be a real mother to her children. It does not have much glory
> to it; there is a lot of grit and grime. But there is no greater
> place of ministry, position, or power than that of a mother.
> —Phil Whisenhunt[7]

There is only one emotion greater than the love of a mother for her newborn. That's the love God has for us, His children. Can anyone, even mothers, begin to comprehend such a great love? A mother's love protects her children. God's love *gave* His only Son to die. If you ever feel as if no one appreciates you or as if you are being taken for granted, think about how deeply you love your children.

Then imagine God loving you more deeply, more powerfully, perfectly—because He does.

From Cindy

One of my books, *The Hope of Refuge*, shares the story of several moms—their strengths, weaknesses, joys, and sorrows. I dedicated the book to my children because each one woke a different part of me, even before I felt him move inside me. When I held each son in my arms, it seemed my very DNA shifted. Without conscious effort each one stirred me with a challenge to be his mom—to become more than I ever was before.

I found strength where weakness had once been. As they grew, they stumbled on weaknesses of mine I hadn't known existed. But because of them and the love I had for them, I discovered that life had unexpected joy. And I learned that where I ended—where my strength, wisdom, and determination failed—God did not.

It's hard to know the best choices to make on a child's behalf—much less to muster the energy, means, and desire to carry out whatever seems to be best. While struggling under the load of everything I was unable to give my children, I learned an important truth: if parents could give their children all that their hearts desire—if we could fill every need they have—they wouldn't need God.

Parents are simply grown-up children. Our powers are limited. But through our faith and prayers, God can fill every gap. And in the process, our children will grow in their own relationships with Him. But while all that is taking place, we get the pleasure of watching them grow and learn and become their own person.

THE GIFTS
OF CHILDREN

Lo, children are an heritage of the LORD:
and the fruit of the womb is his reward.

—PSALM 127:3

From Cindy

From the time my boys were little, I loved doing crafts with them during the holidays. I'd pull out all sorts of items I'd picked up from yard sales or bought on sale throughout the year and let them create. The mess was well worth it when they excitedly held up their masterpieces. As they grew older, their interest in doing crafts began to fade, but I held on to my Christmastime tradition as long as I could.

One Christmas craft they enjoyed for a long time was making dough ornaments. (I've shared the recipe below.) After the holidays you can pack them away with the rest of the ornaments, and every year when you pull out that box of decorations, you'll have a delightful time recalling fond memories.

We had other traditions throughout the year—fireworks and swimming on the Fourth of July, carving pumpkins in the fall, staying up late playing games on New Year's Eve, making special candies and cards on Valentine's Day, hosting Super Bowl celebrations and family birthday parties. But as my sons became teens, they no longer looked forward to our family traditions.

Gathering teenagers to make memories takes an extra bit of creativity (and patience!), regardless of the season. My solution to extending their joy of making something Christmassy was to use food as the craft time. I allowed them to decorate their own gingerbread-men ornaments—one year it was a demolition gingerbread man with a jackhammer in his hand. Other years I let them create gingerbread houses and then munch on their little homes as the holidays progressed.

Whatever your kids' ages, be imaginative and free spirited in your family traditions. They'll love you for it…eventually.

DOUGH ORNAMENT RECIPE

4 cups all-purpose flour
1 cup salt
1½ cups warm water

Mix flour and salt. Slowly add warm water, and stir to form a stiff dough. Press dough to about ⅛" thick, and use cookie cutters to cut out ornaments. Add ornament hooks to the top before baking. Bake at 325 degrees until ornaments have hardened, about 50 minutes. Cool. Decorate using acrylic paints. You may wish to coat them with shellac to help preserve them. (If your kids want to eat the decorations, use an edible recipe and frosting instead of paint. And be sure to skip the shellac!)

From Miriam

When my daughter, Amanda, was about seven years old, she seemed to be constantly underfoot. I never made much headway in the housecleaning with her around.

One day, in an attempt to channel her overabundant energy, I asked if she'd like to bake a cake for her brothers. To my relief she responded with interest. I set out all the utensils, measuring cups, bowls, and ingredients she would need, told her to follow the directions on the box, and instructed her to call me before putting the batter into the oven.

From the time Amanda had been old enough to push a chair up to the counter, she'd been at my side while I baked, watching and helping me. So by now I trusted her with the task.

I hurried upstairs in hopes of getting some work done. I had barely started when Amanda called up to me. I walked to the top of the stairs. "What is it?" I asked as patiently as I could.

"How many cups of the cake mix do I use?"

"All of it, dear."

"Okay," she said. "This must be a *big* cake."

All was quiet for some time, and I accomplished a lot. When my little girl called me to help her put the cake into the oven, I tried not to notice the messy kitchen or the bits of eggshells in the bottom of the bowl. Most of them clung to the sides as we scooped the cake batter into the baking pan. This time it was my treat to lick the bowl.

Later, as her brothers ate the cake, they found more eggshells, along with the plastic Amanda had snipped off the top of the bag and a piece of the box. That's my enthusiastic girl! But with five brothers, she will never live it down.

Today she works at a bakery two days a week and can make a recipe like the one below without any inedible items jumping into the bowl.

Chocolate Coffee Cake

1 box chocolate cake mix
1 box instant vanilla pudding mix
1 cup vegetable oil
4 eggs
1 cup water

Mix all ingredients together. Pour *half* of the batter
into a 9" x 13" cake pan. Then mix the topping
ingredients, and sprinkle half of it on top of the batter.
Then repeat the layers.

Topping:
1 cup brown sugar
2 teaspoons cinnamon
1 cup nuts
1 cup chocolate chips

Preheat oven to 350 degrees. Bake for 40 minutes.
The usual methods of testing a cake for doneness are
inserting a clean toothpick, touching the top lightly,
and seeing if the sides of the cake have pulled free of
the pan, but those don't work well on this cake
because of the gooey chocolate chips in the center
and on the top.

OPPORTUNITY FOR THE TAKING

Do not withhold good from those who
deserve it, when it is in your power to act.

—PROVERBS 3:27, NIV

From Miriam

Loretta, an English friend, was diagnosed with colon cancer and immediately had emergency surgery, but the prognosis wasn't good. She'd
always loved my homemade vegetable soup, so after she came home from
the hospital, I made a batch and took it to her. We had a lovely visit, and
as I left her house, I decided to maintain communication with her while
she recuperated.

We stayed in touch mostly by phone, and she kept me posted on her
condition. She recovered from the surgery and began chemo treatments.

As time went on, I became busy with gardening, canning, yard work,
and tending to my small craft business. When my two school-age children went on summer break, my schedule became more full. As the heat
began to fade, the children returned to school, and I felt bad that I never
followed through with my intentions to visit Loretta. We rarely even
spoke on the phone.

Then one day Loretta's daughter, Elizabeth, stopped by to say her
mother was getting worse.

I prepared Loretta's favorite soup and fresh dinner rolls and took them to her, along with a few jars of homemade goods. As I sat with my friend, guilt washed over me. Loretta had lost her sense of taste, so none of my fresh-baked or canned food really blessed her. I remembered a saying from my childhood: "One little deed done in time is worth more than a thousand good intentions."

Before leaving her home, I prayed for a new way to help my friend. I begged her daughter to call me if there was anything I could do. The next day she stopped by, asking if I'd make her mother some loose-fitting nightgowns. I hurried to the task, thankful for this new opportunity.

A week later Loretta passed away. At her funeral I was humbly honored to see that my friend had chosen one of my homemade gowns for her burial.

Thanks to God's grace, and in spite of my procrastination, my work had blessed Loretta and her children after all.

From Cindy

When I was in my late thirties, I started my day hours before daylight and ended it well after the sun went down. I was raising three sons: one preschooler, one homeschooled seventh grader, and one high schooler who'd just begun honors classes. My days were a tangled array of meeting needs.

Tommy worked sixty hours a week, and my teens needed my help with their schoolwork and with getting them to extracurricular activities. In addition, our preschooler had digestion issues. I have a brother who had the same problem, and he sustained permanent damage because of it. The stress never eased.

By May of that year, I was longing for the seven-hundred-mile road trip we always took in June to visit my parents. I needed to feel my mother's arms around me, hear her words of encouragement, and soak in the sense of respect she radiated. To everyone else I was just Mom doing her best. But to my mother, my value had no limits. I knew I'd leave her home feeling refreshed and strong again.

One night my husband and I stood at the sink washing dishes while our preschooler sat on the floor zipping Matchbox cars across the linoleum.

"Mom," Tyler said, "you should call Grandma."

"I just talked to her a few days ago. She's busy making plans for planting her spring flowers."

He returned to playing with his toys, and I continued my conversation with my husband. When I tucked my son in that night, he repeated his suggestion. Again I waved away the idea.

As Tommy and I were heading out the door the next day to run errands, Tyler came into the foyer. "Mom, you should call Grandma."

My husband looked at me funny. "Maybe you should."

I picked up our youngest son. "I talked to her a few days ago, and we agreed we'd talk again on Tuesday. It's on the calendar. I won't forget."

When Tyler mentioned it again on Sunday afternoon, I was neck deep in helping my oldest son study for finals. And Adam had been diagnosed with a severe case of chickenpox, even though he'd had the vaccine. He was running a fever and was covered in little red blotches.

On Monday night I attended an awards ceremony at my oldest son's school while Tommy watched our preschooler and the teenager with the pox. At the ceremony Justin won five awards—local, countywide, and statewide. Having worked so hard to prepare him for public school, I felt as if I could breathe for the first time in quite a while.

As we walked back into our home, I heard the phone ringing. My husband answered it. "I'm sorry," I heard him say, "but I can't understand you. Who is this?"

A few moments later I heard him speak my dad's name. The horror on my husband's face made my legs go weak.

Tommy hung up the phone and told me to sit down. Then he informed me that my mom had died of a heart attack while planting her spring flowers.

I'd been given several nudges to stop what I was doing and call her.

In my busyness I missed that chance. I'd never once considered that Mom might die in her sixties. Her mother and her mother's mother had lived well into their nineties. She and I had always talked of her and my brother Leston moving in with us when Dad passed. He wasn't sick, but we were going with the probabilities—women usually outlive men.

I'd assumed too much, and my only solace was that we'd taken the time to build and maintain a good relationship over the years—after I was out of my teen years, of course. Back then, she was my safe haven if I needed to complain, whine, or pitch fits. When I matured, I saw her strength and value.

Because her death caught me unprepared, I do my best never to take any relationship or any parting words for granted. As cliché as it sounds, we truly don't know what tomorrow holds—except that God will meet us there and be our strength, our hope, and our *nevertheless*.

ANNUAL QUILT AUCTION

Every man according as he purposeth in
his heart, so let him give; not grudgingly,
or of necessity: for God loveth a cheerful
giver.

—2 CORINTHIANS 9:7

From Cindy

Sitting in Miriam's yard, I sipped a cup of coffee as I watched sunlight
peek over the mountains and fill the valley. Sunlight sparkled off the
dewy grass. The steady *clop* of horses' hoofs against the asphalt softened
as the rigs pulled onto the gravel driveway.

It was a day I'd looked forward to for a year. The annual Amish
school sale. It's a bustling auction with at least four auctioneers selling
various goods at different stations, two makeshift kitchens, a few special-
event tents, and several commercial-sized grills filled with chicken.

Delicious aromas fill the air, as does the sweet sound of families and
friends greeting one another. There is an ocean of Amish men, women,
and children milling about—cooking, helping the auctioneers, bidding,
and eating as time allows. The youth play volleyball and baseball out in
the fields away from the auction area.

The sales from each year's auction support Amish schools in the surrounding districts. So on that beautiful spring day, several districts of

Amish people were attending the school sale, along with hundreds of Englischers.

Cars are parked in a freshly mowed hay field on one side of the road. Buggies sit in a different field with a fenced pasture holding the unharnessed horses. On the far side of the warehouse-type building, several portable potties and sinks are set up.

On the day of this auction, probably a thousand people congregated inside the warehouse-type building used in the family's timber-framing business.

This school sale was a great gift-buying opportunity for me. My readers love the chance to win Amish-made crafts, wall hangings, and quilts. Every Amish person who's made and brought an item to sell receives a percentage of its selling price, so it's one of those win-win situations I'm honored to participate in.

My dad, stepmom, sister, and one brother were there too, along with my husband and one of our sons. We were busy eating and drinking the homemade goods and bidding on everything from handsewn, faceless dolls to birdhouses to carvings to wall hangings to king-sized quilts.

After the crowds went home, the cleanup began. The sun sank behind the mountains, and about the time darkness settled over the land, everything was in sufficient order for supper to begin. About nine o'clock that night, amid soft conversations and bursts of laughter, my husband, youngest son, and I sat at Miriam and Daniel's familiar old oak table and shared a meal with a group of very weary and content Amish folk. Those men and women had worked for weeks to be ready for the auction, and they'd earned enough money to pay the schoolteachers for several districts in the area. They were pleased.

The following day my husband and son headed home in our van, which was loaded to maximum capacity with Amish-made goodies. When I finally tore myself away from my Amish friends a week later, I had two things on my mind—the fun of giving all those items away throughout the year and the expectation of attending next year's auction.

From Miriam

Our community's annual quilt auction is usually held on the second Saturday in May, with the proceeds benefiting our local Amish schools. The auction is open to the public, and approximately two thousand people attend each year.

Having it before Mother's Day gives people the opportunity to pick up a gift for that special motherly someone in their lives. In addition to numerous handcrafted quilts, many other homemade gifts and delicious treats are offered for sale.

As the time draws near, the whole valley is abuzz with preparations. In homes, ladies feverishly quilt. In shops, men build furniture and crafts. In nurseries, gardeners coax potted plants and hanging baskets to bloom in time for the special day.

But no one looks forward to this event quite as much as the children. For weeks before the sale, many of them do odd jobs and chores for a little extra spending money. For them, the biggest decision of the day is what to buy first: a soft pretzel, a fresh doughnut, or something sweet at the candy stand. Rachel's booth is usually among the most popular spots of the day. She owns a dry-goods store in our area, and her gift corner on the day of the auction offers toys, books, and delightful items for all ages.

One year my ten-year-old son worked especially hard to earn money for the upcoming event. He'd spent most of his cash by lunchtime, so he skipped the meal in order to buy me something special for Mother's Day.

I was deeply touched by his sacrifice and selflessness. How God-pleasing this must have been. Our Lord loves a cheerful giver whose heart is as generous as that of a child. When I don't want to give of myself or I don't want to give something away because I'm feeling selfish, I remember two things—that wonderful feeling of freely giving when I was a child and the abundance of what God has given to me over the years.

Do You See What I See?

Do you show contempt for the riches of
his kindness, tolerance and patience, not
realizing that God's kindness leads you
toward repentance?

—ROMANS 2:4, NIV

From Miriam

My English friend Linda came home from work one day, and as she
opened the door, she had to shove the cat aside with her foot. Being greeted
at the end of a tiring day by a friendly cat would be nice, but Linda had
barely made it inside when her furry friend started up with its pleading
meows. The cat would not let up. It kept begging until Linda fed it.

After grabbing a bag of dry cat food and dumping some into a bowl,
she stepped outside and placed it on the porch, finally silencing the per-
sistent feline. As the cat ate, Linda scratched its back a second or two, then
walked away. The cat followed, leaving its food. It rubbed against Linda's
legs as she tried to move.

Sidestepping the little creature, Linda sat in her porch rocker for a
minute of relaxation before starting her own supper. The cat jumped up
on her lap, nudging Linda's chin and begging to be petted.

After a few strokes the cat settled down for a nap. But the minute
Linda got up, the cat was at it again, rubbing against her every time she

took a step. No matter how many times Linda shoved it aside, the cat came back.

After supper Linda and her husband, Rick, sat on the porch swing with the tabby at their feet as they tried to swing. She told him about the pet's antics.

"You know," Rick said, "that cat reminds me of God."

Linda's eyebrows rose.

"We go about our daily routines, trying to do what we want to do, striving to accomplish our goals. And when God tries to get our attention, we tend to shove Him aside, thinking He's getting in our way. But He gently persists until we finally spend time with Him and show Him that we love Him."

From that day on, Linda has looked at her cat with fresh perspective. And she has viewed God with new eyes as well.

From Cindy

While my brother Mark was in school, he worked as a farmhand to earn enough money to buy an old fixer-upper car. He spent summers and weekends baling hay, milking cows, and cleaning barns. His employers, the Zimmermans, stopped by the house on occasion, bragging that he was the best hired hand they'd ever had.

Finally Mark had earned enough money to buy a '57 Plymouth Belvedere at an auction. He bought one in good enough condition to drive off the lot, but he didn't have a driver's license, so Dad drove it home for him. They parked it in a patch of woods near the house, and Mark spent weeks tinkering with the motor, cleaning the upholstery, and waxing it.

I'd never seen my brother happier. He told everyone about his beautiful Plymouth Belvedere.

One afternoon Mr. and Mrs. Zimmerman came by to see the car. I walked next to my brother as he proudly took them up the hill. When the vehicle came in sight, Mr. Zimmerman stopped. He looked at Mark. "You've been kidding us."

A confused look came over Mark's face. "About what?"

"You said you had a jade green car."

"Well, what shade of green would you call it?"

Mr. Zimmerman glanced at his wife. "Mark, that car is pink."

I'd known he was color-blind, but I didn't know he thought the car was green. When my brother looked at me, I saw the hurt in his eyes.

"It's a beautiful pink," I said.

He laughed without mirth. Then he confessed to the Zimmermans that he was color-blind.

They laughed with him and assured him the car was gorgeous, no matter what its color. But my brother never felt the same about the car after that…or, for a long time, about himself.

I've thought about that event a lot over the years, perhaps because one of our sons is also color-blind. Embarrassing moments and lack of confidence are part of the package in our color-conscious world. But that incident brings to my mind a spiritual parallel that clings to me even more.

We don't all see the world in the same colors or shades. We never will. Each generation, culture, class, region, and denomination sees life's issues in varying shades and colors.

If we all saw everything through the same lens, we wouldn't ever be challenged when we're wrong, need to reevaluate our point of view, or seek anyone else's opinion about anything because we'd all think alike.

Seems to me that's when all color would drain from life.

LIGHT FLOODING THE DARK

Then spake Jesus again unto them, saying,
I am the light of the world: he that followeth
me shall not walk in darkness, but shall have
the light of life.

—JOHN 8:12

From Miriam

My husband and sons enjoy hunting. So when autumn finally rolls around, it's time to go shopping for supplies: ammunition, rain gear, flashlights, and chocolate bars.

While the Amish don't use electricity, some battery-operated implements are okay. When LED headlamps hit the market, the boys thought they were the neatest invention, and each had to have one.

At the end of one season's first day, our boys were swapping stories as usual. I overheard one of them say that he had wandered around in the dark woods with rain pouring down on him because he couldn't find his tree stand. To make the situation worse, he had a dim headlamp.

With the light of dawn, he discovered that his flashlight had two more switches for brighter lighting. He was both frustrated at having stumbled around in the dark when he didn't have to and thankful to know about those switches for the next time.

When he said that, I pictured how God's children wander aimlessly in the darkness until we invite Jesus into our lives. We don't even realize what is missing in our lives until we discover Him. And even after He comes in, we squint in the dimness until we learn how to flip on that third switch that enables us to see more clearly. Then we receive the peace and contentment that come with having His love in our hearts.

From Cindy

I love words, always have. They enlighten. Encourage. Entertain. They can lift a heavy load or bury someone under a load. And they often do both whether we're paying attention or not. Words come at us all the time through a lot of sources; they're unavoidable.

I used to tax my poor mom, wanting to know the names for *everything*. She tried to help and often dragged out my dad's *Random House Dictionary* and scoured it for the right word.

Of course, I didn't love all words. As a child, I'd shudder when I heard certain words. One of my most hated words, believe it or not, was *elbow*. Oh, I despised it! I really don't know why, but it sounded as ugly and offensive to me as a curse word.

When I told my mother how much I despised it, she looked at me oddly. A few moments later she nodded that she understood. When I begged her to promise that she would never use that word again, she rubbed her forehead, as if trying to decide whether to honor my request or tell me to go grind feed for the chickens. She studied me, probably thinking how hard it would be to keep such a promise. Finally we made a pact never to use that word unless it was absolutely necessary.

Words have power.

God spoke, and light and entire worlds came into existence. He gave a name to each thing He created, starting with day and night, light and dark.

Through our words we have the power to bring light or dark into our world and the worlds of those around us. What words will you not say for your loved ones' sake? Which ones will you choose to use?

THE STRENGTH
OF WEAKNESS

My strength is made perfect in weakness.
Most gladly therefore will I rather glory in
my infirmities, that the power of Christ may
rest upon me.

—2 CORINTHIANS 12:9

From Cindy

Whenever I visit Miriam, we begin our mornings in her "hiddy"—a secluded spot to rest, pray, and visit with sisters and close friends. Her vegetable garden is mere feet away, and behind it is a huge pasture for the horses. We sit in lawn chairs tucked behind a set of L-shaped lilac bushes, sip fresh-perked coffee, and talk quietly while the earth wakens to a new day.

When time allows, we return to that spot at the end of our day and watch darkness fall, listening to the songs of birds bidding the world good night. Tree frogs, cicadas, and crickets sing boldly. And we occasionally hear my favorite nocturnal bird, chuck-will's-widow.

During some of those quiet, still times, Miriam and I began to talk about our desire to share our lives with our readers—not a list of how-to tips, ten steps to better living, or learning to gain control over yourself, your husband, your children, or your life. We simply wanted to tell our experiences—the tough, fun, encouraging, disappointing, and embarrassing moments—so they might instill a sense of hope, victory, and humor into our readers' days.

With each visit Miriam and I realized a little more how much we wanted to write a book together. We longed to share what we know about connecting with God and shaping our limited talents into successful living—in ourselves, our marriages, our children, and every other relationship. Basically, we wanted to invite our readers into the hiddy with us and tell them what God has told us: *You can do this. You won't get it perfectly right. Only I can do that. You won't fully complete the task at hand. But I can complete it for you.*

We wanted to be transparent but not so much that anyone in our lives, precious or difficult, felt embarrassed or angered by what we'd shared. So we've written honestly and openly, yet cautiously.

Whatever challenges face you, wherever you are in your journey of life, His strength can continually strengthen you. Philippians 4:13 says, "I can do all things through Christ which strengtheneth me." His love can fill you to overflowing. First Thessalonians 3:12 says, "The Lord make you to increase and abound in love one toward another, and toward all men, even as we do toward you."

Perhaps you don't feel worthy of receiving anything for yourself. Shortly after I accepted Christ, I felt so guilty I couldn't even enjoy praying. I kept rehashing every wrong deed I'd ever done. One day, while wallowing in a melancholy state of guilt, I heard these words in my heart: *What did I die for if not for sins?*

I'd heard that concept many times. But in that moment I saw the ridiculousness of lugging my guilt around. Christ was crucified for the very purpose of forgiving us and freeing us from sin and guilt. That revelation brought me great relief.

You are worthy to receive His hope and make a success out of your life for Him. Don't believe God's best is only for your children, friends, spouse, sister, brother, mom, or dad.

Believe it for yourself.

From Miriam

Cindy sat next to me in my craft room as we worked on finding the right format for our book, *Plain Wisdom*. I was still a bit skeptical about our project, feeling insecure about my abilities in this new line of work. At that point I wasn't even certain it was truly God's will.

For our first chapter we wrote "Finding Peace." We each had completed our respective pieces, but we needed a scripture to complete our entry. Cindy searched the Bible on her laptop while I paged through my tattered Bible.

The room was quiet except for the soft *click, click* of Cindy's computer and the occasional rustle of my Bible pages. After searching for some time, we each came up with a verse we thought might work. After reading each other's choice, we looked up and smiled. Out of all sixty-six books of the Bible, 1,189 chapters, and more than thirty-one thousand verses, we had both chosen the exact same scripture: Ecclesiastes 3:1. "To every thing there is a season, and a time to every purpose under the heaven." I considered that an encouraging nudge from God, telling me He was behind our writing this book. And that must have been true, because you have that book in your hands now. But accomplishing the goal was tougher than I'd planned on.

Cindy and I knew we'd have challenges—carving out time amid our busy family lives, working together despite the distance between us, my writing each entry in longhand and mailing them individually to Cindy for her to type up and merge into one master document—but had we known what we'd each face within our families while trying to write, we probably wouldn't have embarked on our journey. Cindy's dad has been ill for several years now, but his health took a harsh turn for the worse. She needed to prepare her home to receive her special-needs brother. My youngest son, Mark, was seriously injured in an accident, and I had to tend to him round the clock for nearly two months. None of those setbacks really tells the exhausting emotional toll of those events. But I think about that encouragement from God time and again, and I know something now that I don't believe I knew then: encouragement from God isn't about assuring us the journey will be easy but that the work accomplished will be fruitful.

Our Final Thoughts

> Yet the Lord will command His lovingkind-
> ness in the daytime, and in the night his song
> shall be with me, and my prayer unto the
> God of my life.
>
> —Psalm 42:8

From Cindy's and Miriam's hearts to yours

It's time for us to say good-bye. Our hearts are overjoyed that you trusted us with some of your time, and we hope something we've shared has benefited you.

As you read our stories, you saw the many differences and similarities between us and our daily lives. In many ways our lifestyles are so different it's hard to understand how we navigated around those things to form a wonderful friendship. When we first began to get to know each other, I (Miriam) had spent so little time among the English that on some occasions I couldn't think of an English word to describe what I wanted to tell Cindy. We know only a few of the same church songs. We don't have movies, travel, or schooling in common.

So what drew us together?

We believe it's the same thing that draws all of us together, regardless of our culture or background—a sense of respect and love. Believers have a kindred spirit that comes from having the same God the Father, God the Son, and God the Holy Spirit.

We hope you've felt that spirit of sisterhood with us as you've read this book. And we pray that you'll find someone special to share your life moments with as we've shared ours with you.

Proverbs 17:17 says, "A friend loveth at all times, and a brother is born for adversity."

Family members can be some of our closest friends. Strangers can become our closest friends. In John 15:15 our own Savior calls Himself our friend. When His lovingkindness surrounds us, it often comes through the vessel of family and friends.

If you're anything like I (Cindy) was throughout most of my adult life, you may not be good at making friends, but I encourage you to ask God to open doors and then put the necessary effort into walking through them. Endure awkward or embarrassing moments when necessary. You'll discover all sorts of interesting things about others and yourself. You'll grow in ways that will strengthen and change you. And you'll open up your heart to new facets of the human experience.

As we pointed out in the entry "Amish Friendship Bread," the best way to have a friend is to be one, and the best way to strengthen a friendship is to do kindnesses when they're not expected.

When your friends aren't perfect, be grateful—because if they were, you'd be the only one in that relationship who wasn't.

When we choose to love one another deeply in spite of our differences, we reap the benefits—because love covers a multitude of sins and faults—theirs and ours (see 1 Peter 4:8).

Behatz Sei Hoffning (Embrace His Hope),
Cindy and Miriam

DISCUSSION GUIDE

1. Have you ever had a friend whose background and experiences were vastly different from yours? How did those differences affect your relationship? In what ways did they make the friendship more difficult? In what ways did they make it more special? What commonalities did you discover in spite of the differences?

2. Did you sense the Holy Spirit speaking to you through one or more of the stories in this book? What message did you glean, and how do you think it will affect you?

3. What was your favorite thing about this book? Learning more about novelist Cindy Woodsmall and her real life? Getting to know Cindy's friend Miriam? Gaining a better understanding of the Amish? Which did you enjoy most: the heartwarming stories, the humor, the recipes, or something else?

4. When Miriam and Cindy met the first time, a humorous incident helped break the ice. Have you experienced an awkward situation that was made more comfortable by a touch of humor? What happened, and what was the result?

5. When Cindy had an extended visit with Miriam, it helped her see life from a different perspective. An unexpected event—a bad storm, an electrical outage, a health issue, or a financial crisis—can have the same effect, altering our daily routines and forcing us to do everyday things a little differently. Such changes to our regular schedules can help us see the important things in life that often get buried under the deluge of our daily responsibilities. Have you ever had such an experience? How did it affect your outlook and priorities?

6. Cindy and Miriam both told stories of families who were blessed by strangers. Have you ever been the recipient of such a blessing? Have you ever had the opportunity to be generous to a stranger? Giving and receiving are both part of God's plan for His children. How can you be a better giver and a more gracious recipient?

7. Miriam wrote, "The right word spoken at the right moment can turn a negative situation into a positive one." Have you ever been in a bad situation that was turned around by a "right word"?

8. Cindy and Miriam wrote about favorite memories around the family table. What are some of your cherished mealtime memories? How often does your family gather at the table to eat? If you'd like to have more mealtime memories with your family, how can you increase their frequency?

9. Miriam told about a time when the Lord answered a "seemingly insignificant" request in a special way. Do you sometimes hesitate to "bother" the Lord by praying about the little things? Have you ever prayed for something that seemed trivial, only to be surprised by the Lord's loving response and abundant provision?

10. Cindy and Miriam shared stories about their parents. They also wrote about their experiences as mothers. What special memories do you have of your mother and father? What are you doing now to instill special memories in your children?

11. Miriam and Cindy talked about the friendship they've developed with each other as well as other friendships they've had. What special friends have you made over the years? What makes those relationships so wonderful? How has God been a friend to you when you've been (or felt) friendless?

12. Miriam wrote, "The best way to strengthen a friendship is to do a kindness when it's not expected." What unexpected kindness can you show to a friend this week?

13. Cindy wrote, "When we pray, we often express a deep desire. If we stop expecting a specific response, we may find the answer." Think

of a time when you prayed for something specific but God's response wasn't the answer you expected. How might your prayers change if you stopped looking for the responses you want and started looking for God's answers?

14. In this book did you read about any customs or traditions (Amish or Englischer) that you would like to incorporate into your own family life?

ACKNOWLEDGMENTS

From Miriam

First I would like to thank Cindy Woodsmall for giving me this opportunity, for opening the doors and leading me through them. Your encouragement always inspires me.

Shannon Marchese, Kathy Ide, and Carol Bartley, our editors. Your instructions are invaluable. I am awed by your wisdom and knowledge. Thanks for your patience.

Steve Laube, our agent. Sincere thanks to you for the effort you poured into this project.

Barbara Putrich, your behind-the-scenes work did not go unnoticed and is much appreciated. Bless you.

A special thanks to Daniel, my husband, for your love and support.

To my sons who lived at home during this writing venture—Mervin, Michael, and Mark. You picked up the slack on the home front and were so very patient.

To my married children—David and Martha, Jacob and Naomi. Thanks for all you've done and for not giving up on me.

And to Mervin and Miriam, who married mere weeks after this book was finally finished and on its way to the printer. Watching your love grow touched my heart.

To my helper and critique partner, my daughter, Amanda. You were always truthful and yet merciful. Your notes of encouragement and I-love-yous were a bigger inspiration than you know.

To my English friend Vanessa Ellis. Thank you for believing in me, for your famous lasagna, for picking up groceries again and again, and for helping me get last-minute items to Cindy. I will be forever grateful.

To both sets of parents, my brothers, sisters, and friends. Thank you for allowing me to use your stories.

To WaterBrook Multnomah Publishing Group—marketing, sales, production, and editorial departments. Thank you, all of you. It's been an honor.

To Gary Gates, our friend and driver, for running to the post office and to other delivery services to help Cindy and me meet deadlines. We'd have been lost without you.

Since this book came through faith and not my own wisdom or understanding, I give all glory to God and my Savior, Jesus Christ.

> I can do all things through Christ which strengtheneth me.
> —Philippians 4:13

From Cindy

To my dear friend Miriam Flaud, for daring to trust me when I saw and believed in the hidden gift, the one you still doubt exists—the gift of sharing stirring truths through beautiful storytelling.

To Barbara Putrich, for keeping up with years of Miriam's hand-written entries and for faithfully changing each one into a Word document, and for all the odd creative tasks you took on as a computer-writing novelist and an Old Order Amish woman worked to write a nonfiction book.

To my friend Kathy Ide, for being there throughout this writing project every time I cried, "Help!" Your skills as a freelance editor are much appreciated, and your sacrifice to me as a friend deserves more thank-yous than I can give.

To my editor, Shannon Marchese, for stepping outside your comfort zone to edit something you hadn't edited in a long time—nonfiction—and for believing I could write in a different genre while bringing a novice writer along with me.

To my line editor, Carol Bartley, for all the things I always look forward to—your ability to see what I cannot, your guidance in honing the work to be its best, and the value you place on my writing.

To each one in the WaterBrook Multnomah Publishing Group—my co-workers and support—THANK YOU!

To my dear friend and critique partner, Marci Burke. You are the best!

To my married sons and their wives—Justin and Shweta, Adam and Erin. You have your own stories of family life full of elation, grief, and all the things in between. Each of you continually brings me joy that I embrace without reservation. I am *so* proud of you.

To Tyler, my youngest. You were a child when I took you on my first writing research trip, and now you're a young man with your own driver's license. To my delight, no matter what mode of transportation we used, how far we went, or how long we stayed, you always traveled well, encouraged me all along the way, and accepted with contentment the dedication that writing requires. My heart aches when I think that our days of traveling together for research and your coming into my office to talk about favorite books, directors, screenwriters, movies, and the fun-yet-taxing school days are drawing to a close.

And last, to my husband. I gratefully say that you are everything I'm not. I thought I loved you when we married. I thought I loved you when we had each child and embarked on another journey. I thought I loved you when you stood beside me during the most difficult of times. I thought I loved you when you were stalwart in your support of my dreams. And today I think I love you as much as I possibly can.

Tomorrow you will prove me wrong.

NOTES

1. American Christian Fiction Writers promotes Christian fiction through developing the skills of its authors, educating them in the market, and serving as an advocate in the traditional publishing industry. For more information, go to www.acfw.com.
2. Gina Ingoglia, *The Big Golden Book of the Wild West: American Indians, Cowboys, and the Settling of the West* (New York: Golden, 1991), 40.
3. For more information on author Connie Stevens, go to www .conniestevenswrites.com/.
4. Global Servants is a worldwide, nonprofit missions and ministry organization. For more information, go to www.globalservants .org/.
5. Charles Austin Miles, "In the Garden," Timeless Truths, Free Online Library, http://library.timelesstruths.org/music/In_the_ Garden/.
6. Copyright 1988 by Carol Wimmer. Used by permission. http:// carolwimmer.com/when-i-say-i-am-a-christian.
7. "Mothers—Wise Sayings About Mothers," SeekFind.net, www .seekfind.net/Mothers.html.

LIST OF RECIPES

MORE TITLES FROM CINDY WOODSMALL

SISTERS OF THE QUILT SERIES

ADA'S HOUSE SERIES

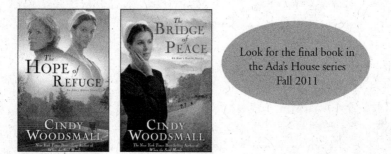

Look for the final book in
the Ada's House series
Fall 2011

Learn more about Cindy,
her books, special contests, sample
chapters, e-newsletters, and more at
www.CindyWoodsmall.com and
www.WaterBrookMultnomah.com

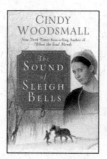